SECULAR HYMNAL

SOLO EDITION: Melodies and Chords to all 144
Secular Hymns in Comfortable, Lowered Keys

"Secular Hymnal - Solo Edition"
by Secretary Michael

ISBN: 978-1-888712-29-2
- 4th Revision -

This book contains the melodies and chords
to all 144 Secular Hymns in comfortable, lowered keys.

All 144 Secular Hymns (both unison/guitar and SATB arrangements)
are available for free download: www.secularhymnal.com

Dedicated to my teacher: Mara Hill

CONTENTS

144 Secular Hymns – Solo Edition
(in Alphabetical Order with Key Signature)

1. A Beauty Hides in Everyone

(From the Solo Edition of the Secular Hymnal - key lowered from C to Bb)

Words & Chords: Secretary Michael

Tune: "Ein Feste Burg" by Martin Luther, 1529
(traditional hymn: "A Mighty Fortress Is Our God")

Lyrics (verse 1):

A beau-ty hides in e-v'ry-one. Our chal-lenge is to bring it out. No mat-ter who or what they've done, they have a beau-ty, we've no doubt. There's beau-ty in the jails, in li-ars with their tales, in cy-nics as they doubt, in bi-gots as they shout. Our chal-lenge is to bring it out.

2. A Long, Long Way We've Come Today

(From the Solo Edition of the Secular Hymnal - key unchanged)

Words & Chords: Secretary Michael

Tune: "Melita" by John Bacchus Dykes, 1861
(traditional hymn: "Eternal Father, Strong to Save")

A long, long way we've come to-day to find a place where we can stay. A

place where we, to - ge - ther here, can live in peace in - stead of fear. So

let us ce - le - brate this day, for we have come a long, long way.

3. A Peaceful Walk

(From the Solo Edition of the Secular Hymnal - key lowered from Eb to D)

Tune: Ralph E. Hudson, 1885
(traditional hymn: "At the Cross")

Words & Chords: Secretary Michael

D   **F#m**   **G**   **A**

1. A peace - ful walk up - on our earth a - way from fear and wrath. We
2. A peace - ful walk up - on our path with o - thers we have told. We

D   **F#m**   **Em**   **A⁷**   **D**

walk a - gain, a - gain, a - gain un - til we have a path. Let us
walk a - gain, a - gain, a - gain un - til we have a road. Let us

D   **A**   **Em**   **A**

walk, walk the walk as we talk,— talk the talk, as we step, step by step find a

D   **G**   **D**   **Bm**

way. When the fear - ful say that we need more guns to - day, we will

Em   **A**   **1. D**   **2. D**

know that there is a bet - ter way. When the way. (A)

4. Accommodating Others

(From the Solo Edition of the Secular Hymnal - key lowered from Eb to D)

Tune: "Penlan" by David Jenkins, 1898
(traditional hymn: "In Heavenly Love Abiding")

Words & Chords: Secretary Michael

Ac - com - mo - dat - ing o - thers is kind of fun to do. It

doe - sn't mean we're toa - dies with - out a point of view. It

takes a skill for learn - ing what o - ther peo - ple need. Ac -

com - mo - dat - ing o - thers lets e - v'ry - one suc - ceed.

5. Achieving Disagreement

(From the Solo Edition of the Secular Hymnal - key unchanged)

Words & Chords: Secretary Michael

Tune: "Angel's Story" by Arthur Henry Mann, 1881
(traditional hymn: "O Jesus I Have Promised")

Lyrics:

A - chiev - ing dis - a - gree - ment can be a plea - sant thing. The al - tos and the bas - ses have dif - f'rent notes to sing. It takes a cer - tain ef - fort to lis - ten and trans - cend the things that we a - gree with to dis - a - gree as friends.

6. All Need To Feel Significant

(From the Solo Edition of the Secular Hymnal - key lowered from E to D)

Words & Chords: Secretary Michael

Tune: "Eventide" by William Henry Monk, 1861
(traditional hymn: "Abide With Me")

Verse lyrics (with chords):

| D | A⁷ | Bm | D | G | A | D |

1. All need to feel sig - ni - fi - cant to - day.
2. Soon - er or la - ter we learn on our own,
3. All need to feel sig - ni - fi - cant to - day.

| Bm | G | D | Em | E⁷ | A | A⁷ |

All need to feel im - por - tant in some way.
those most sig - nifi - cant of - ten are un - known.
It is our job to let them feel that way.

| D | A⁷ | Bm | D | G | B⁷ | Em |

Same goes for chil - dren, teens they need it too.
They're all a - round us, have been all the while,
As we help o - thers be what they can be,

| A | A⁷ | Bm | G | D | A⁷ | D |

All need sig - ni - fi - cance like me and you.
show - ing us how to look a - head and smile.
there is sig - ni - fi - cance in you and me.

7. All Praise to the Troubled

(From the Solo Edition of the Secular Hymnal - key lowered from G to F)

Tune: William Howard Doane, 1875
(traditional hymn: "To God Be the Glory")

Words & Chords: Secretary Michael

1. All praise to the trou-bled, the lost and con-fused, to all schi-zo-phre-nics and those with the blues. All
2. All praise to the out-casts, a-lone and a-drift, bi-po-lars, au-tis-tics with their spe-cial gifts. All

praise to the doubt-ers and those who think free, who o-pen us up to a world that could be. Spin a
praise to the ar-tists in whose fan-ta-sies we learn that there's more to the world than we see. Spin a

REFRAIN

round, spin a round, 'til we're no long-er bound. Spin a round, spin a round, 'til we're way off the ground. All

praise to the trou-bled who help us to see, and o-pen us up to a world that could be.

8. All the Seven Deadly Sins

(From the Solo Edition of the Secular Hymnal - key lowered from Bb to A)

Words & Chords: Secretary Michael

Tune: traditional folk song
(traditional hymn: "Just a Closer Walk With Thee")

Lyrics (lines 1-4, measures 1-4):

0. All the Se - ven Dead-ly Sins	come to vi - sit now and then.____
2. **Glut - to - ny** is kind of sweet	if it has e-nough to eat.____
4. **Pride** comes sing-ing to us all:	"Mir - ror, mir-ror on the wall."____
6. **Sloth** just sits there on its butt.	Half the time it won't show up.__

Lyrics (measures 5-8):

Real - ly don't want them to stay,____	but a short lit - tle chat is o - kay.
Had nine do - nuts on a plate.____	I took one, turned my head, it took eight.
Not con-tent that this will do,____	we're re - ques - ted to all sing it too.
Tried -to fill it with de - light.____	It just sat there and grum-bled "Yea, right."

Lyrics (measures 9-12):

1. **Wrath**'s the one I fear the most.	Ang - ry e - ven o - ver toast.____
3. **En - vy** has no beef with me.	Stuff I have is al - most free.____
5. **Greed** is al - ways worth a laugh.	Once I cut an orange in half.____
7. **Lust** is in a dif - f'rent league.	I have al - ways been in - trigued.__

Lyrics (measures 13-16):

Spew - ing out con - tempt all day,____	How I wish it would just go a - way.
But for those with wealth ga - lore,____	it ob - ses - ses to have e - ven more.
"Greed, there's one for me and you."____	Greed re - plied: "Why take one when there's two?"
But un - for - tu - na - t'ly,____	Lust has not been in-trigued with__ me.

9. Assuming There's Peace

(From the Solo Edition of the Secular Hymnal - key lowered from G to F)

Tune: "Lyons" by Johann Michael Haydn, 1770
(traditional hymn: "O Worship the King")

Words & Chords: Secretary Michael

As - sum - ing there's peace, when real - ly there's none, as -

sum - ing there's peace just might help___ get it done. By

trust - ing and talk - ing to e - ver - y - one, as -

sum - ing there's peace just might help___ get it done.

10. "Bad" is Not a Name

(From the Solo Edition of the Secular Hymnal - key lowered from Dm to Cm)

Tune: "Picardy" (traditional French)
(traditional hymn: "Let All Mortal Flesh Keep Silence")

Words & Chords: Secretary Michael

1. "Bad" is not a name for a wo - man. "Bad" is not a name for a man.
2. "Bad" is not a name for a hus - band. "Bad" is not a name for a wife.
3. "Bad" is not a name for the hun - gry. "Bad" is not a name for the poor.

"Bad" is not a name for a peo - ple. "Bad" is not a name for a land.
"Bad" is not a name for a per - son caught in the ma - chi - n'ry of life.
"Bad" is not a name for the lone - ly who don't want to live a - ny - more.

REFRAIN

"Bad" is just a name for that which cau - ses pain,

not for a - ny vic - tim it claims.

11. Because Violence Can't End Violence

(From the Solo Edition of the Secular Hymnal - key unchanged)

Tune: "Gendarmes' Duet" by Jacques Offenbach, 1867
Adapted by the U.S. Marine Corps, 1919
(traditional hymn: "From the Halls of Montezuma")

Words & Chords: Secretary Michael

1. Be-cause vio-lence can't end vi - o-lence, we re-fuse to march a - long. Be-cause
2. Be-cause ha-tred can't end ha - tred, we re-fuse to march a - long. Be-cause

vio - lence can't end vi - o-lence, we will sing a dif-f'rent song. There are
ha - tred can't end ha - tred, we will sing a dif-f'rent song. There are

ways to change be - ha - vior; tea-chers do it e - v'ry day. Be-cause
ways to change be - ha - vior; par-ents do it e - v'ry day. Be-cause

vio - lence can't end vi - o-lence, we choose PEACE to be our way.
ha - tred can't end ha - tred, we choose LOVE to be our way.

12. Borders, Boundaries, Walls and Fences

(From the Solo Edition of the Secular Hymnal - key lowered from C to Bb)

Words & Chords: Secretary Michael

Tune: "Borders, Boundaries, Walls and Fences" by Secretary Michael
(from the musical "Twimfina")

Lyrics:

Bor - ders, boun - d'ries, walls and fen - ces, one by one they'll dis - ap - pear.

All our so - called dif - fer - en - ces, these are things we do not fear. Don't

talk a - bout ho - nor, don't talk a - bout pride. Don't start wa - ving flags,_ we won't pick a side. Don't
talk a - bout trea - son, the word is a lie. We're not "them and us",_ we're just "you and I". In

threa - ten with spir - its be - low or a - bove, we're pro - tec - ted by sci - ence, pro - tec - ted by love. The
lov - ing the world we're not leav - ing you.__ We hold out our hands, we want you to come too. The

world is our fa - mi - ly, we're not a - fraid! The world is our fa - mi - ly, we're not a - fraid! The
world is our fa - mi - ly, we're not a - fraid! The world is our fa - mi - ly, we're not a - fraid! The

world is our fa - mi - ly, we're not a - fraid! The world is our fa - mi - ly, we're not a - fraid! Don't
world is our fa - mi - ly, we're not a - fraid! The world is our fa - mi - ly, we're not a - fraid!__

Walls and fen - ces, dif - fer - en - ces, we are not a - fraid!

13. Building a Door

(From the Solo Edition of the Secular Hymnal - key lowered from G to F)

Words & Chords: Secretary Michael

Tune: "St. Catherine" by Henri F. Henry, 1864
(traditional hymn: "Faith Of Our Fathers")

Build - ing a door____ through e - v'ry wall. It takes some skill, a ham - mer and saw. Build - ing a door,____ we know____ the way. Let's build a door right here____ to - day. Let's build a door and when it's done, o - pen it up to e - v'ry one.

14. Climbing Up The Ladder

(From the Solo Edition of the Secular Hymnal - key lowered from D to C)

Words & Chords: Secretary Michael

Tune: "Nicaea" by John Bacchus Dykes, 1861
(traditional hymn: "Holy, Holy, Holy")

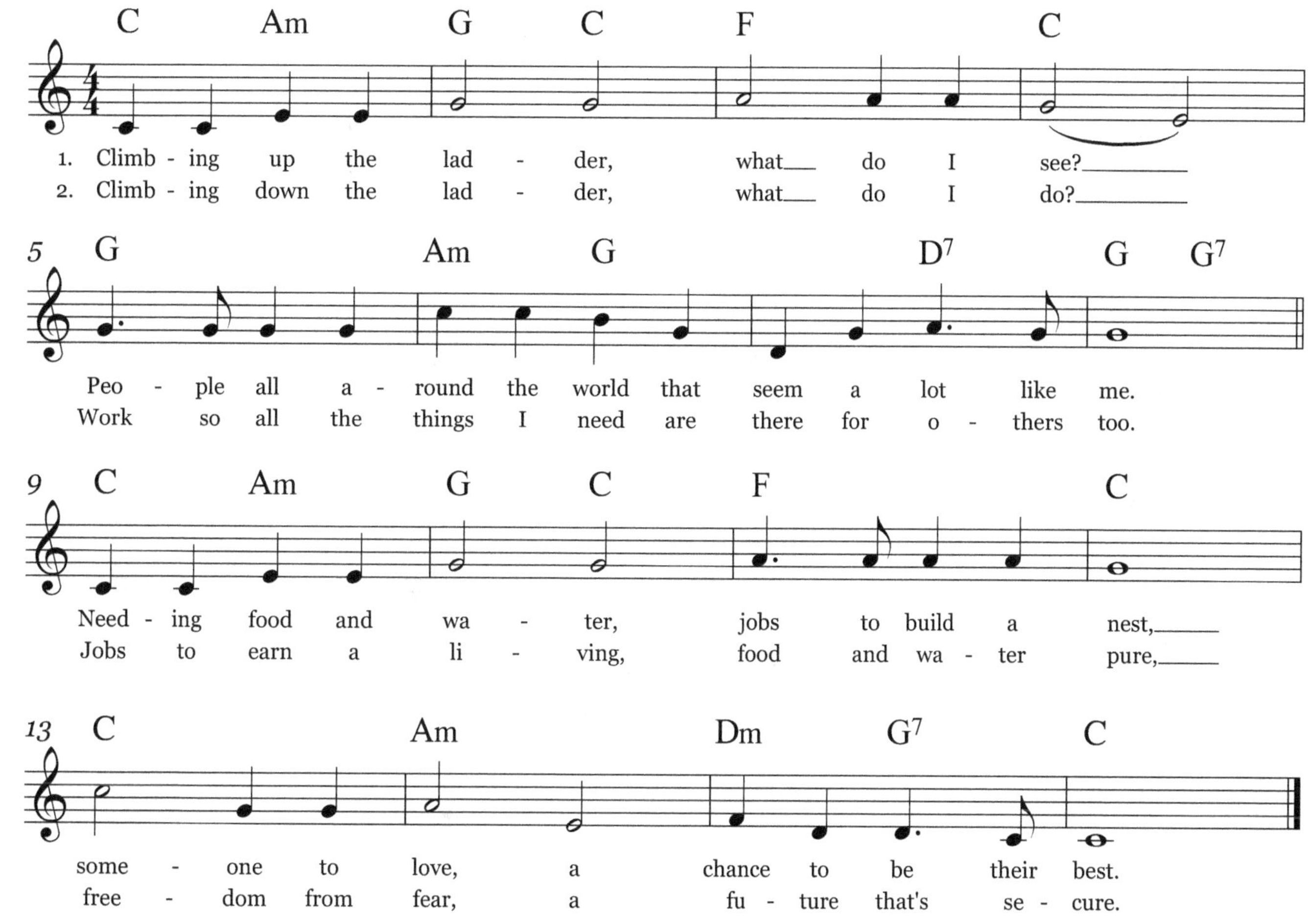

C Am G C F C
1. Climb - ing up the lad - der, what___ do I see?___
2. Climb - ing down the lad - der, what___ do I do?___
5 G Am G D7 G G7
Peo - ple all a - round the world that seem a lot like me.
Work so all the things I need are there for o - thers too.
9 C Am G C F C
Need - ing food and wa - ter, jobs to build a nest,___
Jobs to earn a li - ving, food and wa - ter pure,___
13 C Am Dm G7 C
some - one to love, a chance to be their best.
free - dom from fear, a fu - ture that's se - cure.

15. Climbing Up The Mountain

(From the Solo Edition of the Secular Hymnal - key lowered from F to Eb)

Tune: "Wye Valley" by James Mountain, 1876
(traditional hymn: "At the Name of Jesus")

Words & Chords: Secretary Michael

| Eb | Bb | Cm | Gm | Fm | Bb | Eb |

Climb - ing up the moun - tain, how I want to stop.

| Eb | Bb | Cm | | Bb | F7 | Bb |

But I keep on climb - ing, climb - ing to the top.

| Eb | | Ab | Eb | Fm | Cm | Bb |

Will I e - ver get there? Chance is ve - ry small.

| Eb | G7 | Cm | F7 | Eb | Bb7 | Eb |

But if I stop climb - ing, there's no chance at all.

16. Come Live With Us

(From the Solo Edition of the Secular Hymnal - key lowered from F to D)

Words & Chords: Secretary Michael

Tune: "Come Live With Us" by Secretary Michael
(from the musical "Twimfina")

Come live with us. Come live with us. Ac - cept e - v'ry -

bo - dy and live thus. Come live with us. Come live with us. For

we live in a Love Thy Neigh-bor world. We live in a Love Thy Neigh-bor world.

We live in a Love Thy Neigh-bor world. Come live with us.

17. Communication is the Answer

(From the Solo Edition of the Secular Hymnal - key lowered from G to Eb)

Words & Chords: Secretary Michael

Tune: "Coronation" by Oliver Holden, 1793
(traditional hymn: "All Hail the Power of Jesus' Name")

Eb · Cm · Ab · Bb · Ab · Bb · Eb

1. Com - mu - ni - ca - tion   is   the   an - swer,   let   the   ques - tions   come.   The
2. A   lone - ly   **lob - ster**   asks   for   help,   the   hel - per   shouts   "Ja   Wohl!"*   Yes
3. An   an - gry   **aard - vark**   asks   for   help,   the   hel - per   shouts   "Ja   Wohl!"   Yes
4. A   hope - less   **ham - ster**   asks   for   help,   the   hel - per   shouts   "Ja   Wohl!"   Yes
5. Come   lob - sters,   aard - varks,   ham - sters,   hu - mans,   e - v'ry - one   we   know,   and

Cm · Bb · Eb · Cm · F7 · Bb

har - dest   pro - blems   in   the   world,   we'll   solve   them   one   by   one.   The
I   can   help   cuz   'lone - ly'   is   a   lan - guage   that   I   know.   Yes
I   can   help   cuz   'an - gry'   is   a   lan - guage   that   I   know.   Yes
I   can   help   cuz   'hope - less'   is   a   lan - guage   that   I   know.   Yes
learn   the   ma - ny   lan - gua - ges   so   all   of   us   can   grow.   Com -

Eb · Ab · Bb · Eb

har - dest   prob - lems   in   the   world,   we'll   solve   them   one   by   one.
I   can   help   cuz   'lone - ly'   is   a   lan - guage   that   I   know.
I   can   help   cuz   'an - gry'   is   a   lan - guage   that   I   know.
I   can   help   cuz   'hope - less'   is   a   lan - guage   that   I   know.
mu - ni - ca - tion   is   the   an - swer,   "Ja,   Ja,   Ja,   Ja   Wohl!"

* "Ja Wohl" (pronounced "ya vole") is a German expression meaning "Yes Indeed"

18. Crank and Sprocket

(From the Solo Edition of the Secular Hymnal - key lowered from C to Bb)

Words & Chords: Secretary Michael

Tune: "Easter Hymn" from the *Lyra Davidica* collection of 1708
(traditional hymn: "Jesus Christ is Risen Today")

1. Crank and sproc- ket, chain and wheel. Chug- ga, chug- ga, chug, chug-ga boom boom boom.
2. Head and shoul- ders, knees and toes. Chug- ga, chug- ga, chug, chug-ga boom boom boom.

Spark plug, pis- ton, valve and seal. Chug- ga, chug- ga, chug, chug- ga boom boom boom.
Eyes and ears, a mouth and nose. Chug- ga, chug- ga, chug, chug- ga boom boom boom.

REFRAIN

My ma- chine has ne- ver strayed, ne- ver, ne- ver, ne- ver dis- o- beyed.

Does ex- act- ly as it's made._ Chug- ga, chug- ga, chug- ga, chug-ga boom boom boom.

19. Disassemble Every Gun

(From the Solo Edition of the Secular Hymnal - key lowered from D to C)

Tune: "Nettleton", 1813
(traditional hymn: "Come Thou Fount of Every Blessing")

Words & Chords: Secretary Michael

Dis - as - sem - ble e - v'ry gun and dis - as - sem - ble e - v'ry fear. Then go

scat - ter all the pie - ces so they ne - ver re - ap - pear. Do not

sell them, do not hide them, do not give them a - way. Scat - ter

all the lit - tle pie - ces then be - gin a new day.

20. Diversity in Thought

(From the Solo Edition of the Secular Hymnal - key lowered from F to Eb)

Words & Chords: Secretary Michael

Tune: "Rhosymedre" by John Edwards, 1840
(traditional hymn: "My Song Is Love Unknown")

Di - ver - si - ty in thought is some - thing quite pro - found. It

can't be taught or bought. It on - ly can be found by

turn - ing our - selves 'round and 'round and in - side out and

out - side in and down - side up and up - side down.

21. Don't Choose Sides

(From the Solo Edition of the Secular Hymnal - key lowered from Bb to A)

Tune: "Salve Regina" Hermann of Reichenau, c. 1050
(traditional hymn: "Hail Holy Queen Enthroned Above")

Words & Chords: Secretary Michael

A	E F#m Bm A E7 A

1. There are cer - tain to - pics that di - vide. Don't Choose Sides. Let's_
2. There are times when feel - ings can col - lide. Don't Choose Sides. Let's_

E F#m Bm A E7 A	A D E7 A

choose to be where peace re - sides. Don't Choose Sides. No op - po - nents, on - ly friends.
choose to be where peace re - sides. Don't Choose Sides. Spread the word so all can see

F#m D B7 E A	F#m Bm7/E A

No more los - ses, no more wins. That's the way that peace be - gins.
on both sides hu - ma - ni - ty. That's our chal - lenge, you and me.

A D B E7 A	F#m E7 A

Don't Choose Sides. Don't Choose Sides. Choose to be where peace re - sides.
Don't Choose Sides. Don't Choose Sides. Choose to be where peace re - sides.

PD *All works by Secretary Michael have been placed in the
Public Domain. They may be freely copied and performed.*

22. Don't Know How I Got Here

(From the Solo Edition of the Secular Hymnal - key lowered from Bb to A)

Tune: "Ville Du Havre" (Harbor City) by Philip Paul Bliss, 1876
(traditional hymn: "It Is Well With My Soul")

Words & Chords: Secretary Michael

Don't know how I got here but here___ I___ am. And
all that I have is a plan. Ab - surd as it
seems and what - e - ver it means, I will stay and do the
best that I can. Here I am. Here I

Here I am.

am. I will stay and do the best that I can. Here I can.

Here I am.

23. Each Little Raindrop

(From the Solo Edition of the Secular Hymnal - key lowered from Eb to C)

Words & Chords: Secretary Michael

Tune: "Sutra Hymn" by Secretary Michael

Each lit - tle rain - drop drop - ping in mud___ might bring a ter - ri - ble flood.

Each lit - tle peb - ble tum - bling with pride___ might bring a ter - ri - ble slide.

Lit - tle plea - sures that we take that ne - ver cause of - fense,___

if so done by e - v'ry - one, the strife would be im - mense.___

Each lit - tle plea - sure lead - ing to strife,___ might bring a ter - ri - ble life.

24. Education is our Destination

(From the Solo Edition of the Secular Hymnal - key unchanged)

Words & Chords: Secretary Michael

Tune: *"Warrenton"* (from the Sacred Harp book)
(traditional hymn: "Come Thou Fount of Every Blessing")

C Cmaj7 F C C Am F G C

1. E - du - ca - tion is our de - sti - na - tion! Choo- choo! Chug-ga-Chug-ga! Here we come!
2. Come a - board and join the ce - le - bra - tion! Choo choo! Chug-ga-Chug-ga! Here we come!

5 C Cmaj7 F C Am F G C

Join us on the train of li - ber - a - tion! Choo- choo! Chug-ga-Chug-ga! Here we come! Here we
On the train to get an e - du - ca - tion! Choo- choo! Chug-ga-Chug-ga! Here we come! Here we

REFRAIN

9 Am G F C Am F G C

come, all the stu-dents of each and e - v'ry na - tion! Choo- choo! Chug-ga-Chug- ga! Here we come! On the

13 Am G F C Am F G C

train to an o - pen and an e - qual e - du - ca - tion. Choo- choo! Chug-ga-Chug- ga! Here we come!

25. Every Space for Every Face

(From the Solo Edition of the Secular Hymnal - key lowered from D to C)

Tune: "Salzburg" by Jacob Hintze, 1678
(traditional hymn: "At the Lamb's High Feast We Sing")

Words & Chords: Secretary Michael

E - v'ry space for e - v'ry face. E - v'ry flow - er for e - v'ry vase.

E - v'ry run - ner for e - v'ry race. E - v'ry al - to, te - nor, bass.

No more jobs__ saved just for some. E - v'ry job for e - v'ry - one.

No more stay - ing in one place. E - v'ry space for e - v'ry face.

26. Everybody Has Their Issues

(From the Solo Edition of the Secular Hymnal - key unchanged)

Words & Chords: Secretary Michael

Tune: "There is a Balm in Gilead"
(a traditional African-American spiritual)

E - v'ry-bo - dy has their is - sues that oc - cu-py their mind.____

E - v'ry-bo - dy has their is - sues that come from time to time. It

could be fear or long - ing, de - pres - sion or con - tempt, re -

gret or shame or an - ger, there's no one who's ex - empt, for:

E - v'ry-bo - dy has their is - sues that oc - cu-py their mind.____

E - v'ry-bo - dy has their is - sues that come from time to time.

27. Everyone Must Make a Living

(From the Solo Edition of the Secular Hymnal - key lowered from F to D)

Tune: "Pleading Savior" by Joshua Leavitt (c. 1830)
(traditional hymn: "Sing of Mary")

Words & Chords: Secretary Michael

E - v'ry - one must make a li - ving, e - v'ry - one must make ends meet.

Tea - cher, prea - cher, en - ter - tai - ner, e - v'ry - one needs food to eat.

Praise to the wor - ker, praise to the job.___ Praise to the far - mer and the corn on the cob.

E - v'ry - one must make a li - ving, e - v'ry - one de - serves a job.

28. Everything's Changing

(From the Solo Edition of the Secular Hymnal - key unchanged)

Words & Chords: Secretary Michael

Tune: "Consolation" by Felix Mendelssohn, 1834
(traditional hymn: "Still, Still With Thee")

E - v'ry - thing's chang - ing, and we are chang - ing too.

"Young" be - comes "old", and "old" is born a - new.

All of our dreams for man - kind could come true.

It all de - pends on what we do.

29. For Those Who Have Beliefs Bizarre

(From the Solo Edition of the Secular Hymnal - key lowered from Dm to Bm)

Words & Chords: Secretary Michael

Tune: "Ye Banks and Braes" - a Scottish folk melody
(traditional hymn: "We Cannot Measure How You Heal")

Bm   G   Bm   G

For those who have beliefs bi - zarre, we'll

5   Bm   G   Em   A⁷

al - ways love you for who you are. Al -

9   Bm   G   Bm   G

though your thoughts seem sad and strange we'll

13   Bm   G   A⁷   D

ne - ver leave you or force you to change. When

17   F#m   Bm   F#m   Bm

thoughts, like can - cer, go a - stray they

21   G   Em   A⁷

grow and grow and so we say: For

25   Bm   G   Bm   G

those who have be - liefs bi - zarre, we'll

29   Bm   G   A⁷   D

al - ways love you for who you are.

30. For What I've Done

(From the Solo Edition of the Secular Hymnal - key lowered from F to Eb)

Tune: Louis Lambillotte, c. 1840
(traditional hymn: "Come Holy Ghost")

Words & Chords: Secretary Michael

Bb **Eb** **Bb** **Eb** **Cm**

For what I've done and failed to do, I ask for-

Gm **Ab** **Bb** **Bb7** **Eb**

give - ness from you. For all the pain

Bb **Cm** **Gm** **Ab** **Bb**

I've put you through, I ask for - give - ness from

Gm **Ab** **Bb** **Eb**

you for what I've done and failed to do.

31. Go Further Farther

(From the Solo Edition of the Secular Hymnal - key lowered from Eb to C)

Words & Chords: Secretary Michael

Tune: "Dundee" from the Scottish Psalter, 1615
(traditional hymn: "O God of Bethel By Whose Hand")

Go fur - ther, far - ther past the bor - ders, up the high - est hill.

Then, stand - ing on that high - est hill, go fur - ther, far - ther still.

Go fur - ther, far - ther off to pla - ces ne - ver gone be - fore.

Then, hav - ing reached that fi - nal door, go fur - ther, far - ther more.

32. Going Up, Going Up

(From the Solo Edition of the Secular Hymnal - key lowered from G to F)

Words & Chords: Secretary Michael

Tune: "McDaniel" by Charles Hutchinson Gabriel, 1914
(traditional hymn: "Since Jesus Came Into My Heart")

"Go-ing up, go-ing up, go-ing up, go-ing up" the old e - le-va-tor would say. "Go-ing

up, go-ing up, go - ing up, go-ing up" as if there were no o - ther way. So

when you are start-ing to drown with no one to help you a - round. "Go - ing

up, go - ing up, go - ing up, go-ing up" will help you get back on the ground.

33. Grief Has Got To Take Its Time

(From the Solo Edition of the Secular Hymnal - key unchanged)

Tune: "Toplady" by Thomas Hastings, 1830
(traditional hymn: "Rock of Ages")

Words & Chords: Secretary Michael

Grief has got to take its time, has to pu – ri – fy the mind. Has to

wash a – way the pain. Has to cleanse and heal the brain. There's a

rea – son, there's a rhyme. Grief has got to take its time.

34. Happy Be

(From the Solo Edition of the Secular Hymnal - key lowered from G to Eb)

Tune: "Trust in Jesus" by William James Kirkpatrick, 1882
(traditional hymn: "Tis So Sweet To Trust In Jesus")

Words & Chords: Secretary Michael

1. Hap - py be de - vo - ted tea - chers, gi - ving us a fu - ture bright.
5. Hap - py be our strug - gling ar - tists, draw - ing out our beau - ty.
9. Hap - py be po - lice and fire,___ sav - ing us when things go wrong.

2. Hap - py be our health - care work - ers, car - ing for us day and night.
6. Hap - py those who work for peace,___ voic - ing our hu - ma - ni - ty.
10. Hap - py be the buy - ers, sel - lers, help - ing keep our en - gine strong.

3. Hap - py be our good em - ploy - ers, mak - ing op - por - tu - ni - ties.
7. Hap - py those who care for chil - dren, giv - ing us our de - sti - ny.
11. Hap - py those who work in sci - ence, guid - ing us as we pro - gress.

4. Hap - py be to all our work - ers, shar - ing their best e - ner - gies.
8. Hap - py those who pay their tax - es, fund - ing our so - ci - e - ty.
12. Hap - py be to all our peo - ple, all de - serv - ing hap - pi - ness.

35. Harvesting Hunger

(From the Solo Edition of the Secular Hymnal - key lowered from F to D)

Words & Chords: Secretary Michael

Tune: "Arizona" by Robert Henry Earnshaw (1856-1929)
(traditional hymn: "Lord Of All Being")

Har - vest - ing hun - ger is my fate.
Dish - es of no - thing on my plate.
With - out an e - du - ca - tion,
I'll har - vest hun - ger from now on.

36. I am a Terrorist

(From the Solo Edition of the Secular Hymnal - key lowered from F to D)

Words & Chords: Secretary Michael

Tune: "Trentham" by Robert Jackson, 1888
(traditional hymn: "Breathe On Me")

D — G — D

1. I am a ter - ror - ist. Now_____
2. So will you seat me here? Or will you
3. May - be I'm plain ol' me. May - be I'm

G — A⁷ — D

I'm a saint. I_____ am this and
seat me there? At_____ a desk? Or
some - one strange. Hard_____ to know just

G — Em — D — A⁷ — D

I am that and now_____ I ain't.
on a throne? Or in an e - lec - tric chair?
who is who be - cause_____ peo - ple change.

37. I am the Captain of My Boat

(From the Solo Edition of the Secular Hymnal - key lowered from G to F)

Words & Chords: Secretary Michael

Tune: George Coles, 1883
(traditional hymn: "A Poor Wayfaring Man of Grief")

F Dm Gm C⁷ F Dm Gm C⁷

1. I___ am___ the cap - tain of my boat on a calm, a calm___ and peace - ful sea. I
2. There are e - qual cap - tains, e - qual boats___ that ne - ver sail___ and ne - ver float. On___

5 F Dm Gm A⁷ Dm F/C C⁷ F F D⁷

am___ the cap - tain of my boat on a calm, a calm___ and peace ful sea. With___ waves so still___ I'm
stor - my seas___ with wind and hail___ the boats get smashed and cap - tains jailed. There are cap tains who___ are

10 Gm C⁷ F Dm Gm C⁷ F Dm

sel - dom ill.___ With stars and sun___ my work gets done. I___ am the cap - tain
just like me___ who die up - on___ a vio - lent sea. So___ cre - dit not___ my

14 Gm A⁷ Dm F/C C⁷ F

of my boat on a calm, a calm___ and peace - ful sea.___
boat or me but a calm, a calm___ and peace - ful sea.___

38. I Declare A Brand-New Me

(From the Solo Edition of the Secular Hymnal - key lowered from F to D)

Words & Chords: Secretary Michael

Tune: "Cymraeg" by Robert Lowry, 1876
(traditional hymn: "Here Is Love Vast As the Ocean")

Lyrics:

I de-clare a brand-new me,— not the one I used to be. Not the
one who felt a-shamed. Not the one who lost the game. I have
changed, I have ad-vanced, now I need a se-cond chance. From my
past I now am free.— I de-clare a brand-new me.

39. I Have a Garden in the Park

(From the Solo Edition of the Secular Hymnal - key lowered from F to D)

Words & Chords: Secretary Michael

Tune: "Solid Rock" by William Batchelder Bradbury, 1863
(traditional hymn: "My Hope Is Built On Nothing Less")

I have a gar - den in the park where chil - dren play and dog - gies bark. Where home - less peo - ple just like me can sit a while and re - ver - ie. Un - til the end when skies go dark and I will have to dis - em - bark, I have a gar - den in the park.

40. I Have a Puzzle of the World

(From the Solo Edition of the Secular Hymnal - key lowered from D to C)

Tune: "St. Peter" by Alexander Robert Reinagle, 1836
(traditional hymn: "How Sweet the Name of Jesus Sounds")

Words & Chords: Secretary Michael

C　Am　G⁷　C　Dm　F　G

I have a puz - zle of the world I work on with - out cease. But

Dm　F　G　Am　F　G⁷　C

I can ne - ver get it done 'cuz o - thers have a piece. So

C　Am　G⁷　C　Dm　F　G

now I al - ways ask for help, and help out e - v'ry - one. 'Cuz

Dm　F　G　Am　F　G⁷　C

if we do not share the task, we'll ne - ver get it done.

41. I Once Was So Certain

(From the Solo Edition of the Secular Hymnal - key lowered from G to F)

Tune: "Lourdes Hymn"
(traditional hymn: "Immaculate Mary")

Words & Chords: Secretary Michael

1. I once was so cer - tain, so right - eous, so strong. But
2. To - day I'm not cer - tain, not right - eous, not strong. The

now I can see that I had it all wrong. All
world would be bet - ter if you came a - long. A -

wrong, all wrong, I had it all wrong. All
long, a - long, if you came a - long. A -

wrong, all wrong, I had it all____ wrong.
long, a - long, if you came a - long.

42. I Surrender

(From the Solo Edition of the Secular Hymnal - key unchanged)

Words & Chords: Secretary Michael

Tune: "Surrender" by Winfield Scott Weeden, 1896
(traditional hymn: "I Surrender All")

REFRAIN

I sur-ren - der, I sur-ren - der, I sur-ren-der my use - less things.

I sur-ren - der, I sur-ren - der, I sur-ren-der for the peace it brings.

VERSES

1. All my shi - ny things, jew - el - ry and rings.
2. Ho - nors I have won, things that I have done,
3. Wealth mis-un - der - stood, earned as much I could.

Let them go,___ there is no___ hap - pi - ness they bring.
All this pride I push a - side, it's not who I've be - come.
Now I don't care, let it go where it will do some good. (I surrender...)

43. I Think I Could Work in a Castle

(From the Solo Edition of the Secular Hymnal - key unchanged)

Words & Chords: Secretary Michael

Tune: Helen Howarth Lemmel, 1922
(traditional hymn: "Turn Your Eyes Upon Jesus")

1. I think I could work in a cas - tle by sweep-ing and mop-ping the floors. I
2. I think I could work in a fac - t'ry by do - ing what - e - ver they need. I'd

would-n't mind be - ing a vas - sal. I'm not a - bove me - ni - al chores.
find it all quite sa - tis - fac - t'ry, and I'd do my best to suc - ceed.

Cas - tle bells I could ring, ring, or in the roy'l choir I could sing. I'd be
Clean - ing all that needs clean - ing, or pick-ing up gar-bage to toss. I'd be

hap - py do - ing most a - ny - thing cuz I've learned I don't need to be king.
hap - py do - ing most a - ny - thing cuz I've learned I don't need to be boss.

44. I Think I'm Right

(From the Solo Edition of the Secular Hymnal - key lowered from A to G)

Words & Chords: Secretary Michael

Tune: George Frederick Root, 1870
(traditional hymn: "Come to the Savior, Make No Delay")

I think I'm right but I could be wrong. Show me the facts and I'll come a-long.

May - be there's some - thing I do not see. A pos - si - bi - li - ty.

Yes there is a pos - si - bi - li - ty. Yes there is a pos - si - bi - li - ty.

May - be there's some - thing I do not see. A pos - si - bi - li - ty.

45. I Will Look and I Will See

(From the Solo Edition of the Secular Hymnal - key lowered from G to F)

Tune: "Sagina" by Thomas Campbell, 1825
(traditional hymn: "And Can It Be?")

Words & Chords: Secretary Michael

I will_____ look, and I_____ will_____ see the
beau - ty_____ of hu - ma - ni - ty.
Clear as a page in a pic - ture book. Just
o - pen up_____ and take a look.
We can - not see un - less_____ we look._____ So
look, look, look, look, look, look, look, look, look, look, look, look, look. Yes
I will look, and I will see, the
beau - ty of hu - ma - ni - ty. Yes, ty.

46. If We're Not the Ones

(From the Solo Edition of the Secular Hymnal - key unchanged)

Words & Chords: Secretary Michael

Tune: "Hanson Place" by Robert Lowry, 1864
(traditional hymn: "Shall We Gather at the River")

If we're not the ones who do it, ne - ver take the time to view it,

ne - ver strug - gle to pur - sue it, then it pro - ba - bly won't get___ done.

Peace is al - ways worth pur - su - ing, re - gard - less of the con - flict that is brew - ing.

So let's pick a stra - te - gy of do - ing, then work and___ work 'til it's done.

47. I'm Marching, Marching

(From the Solo Edition of the Secular Hymnal - key lowered from G to F)

Tune: "Old Hundredth" by Louis Bourgeois, 1551
(traditional hymn: "Praise God From Whom All Blessings Flow")

Words & Chords: Secretary Michael

	F	Dm	B♭	F	
1.	I'm march - ing,	march - ing	on my	trail.	I
2.	While march - ing	on my	path one	day,	I
3.	They give to	me their	hand to	hold.	To

	Dm	B♭	Gm	C	
	won't get lost,	I will	not fail.	I've
	find that there's	a dif - frent	way,	with
	reach it I	must leave	my road.	If

	C	B♭	F	
	thought things out,	I've done the	math.	I
	dif - frent peo - ple,	dif - frent	views,	with
	peace and love is	to pre - vail,	we

	Dm	Gm	C7	F
	know I'm on the	per - fect	path.
	dif - frent feet in	dif - frent	shoes.
	some - times must march	off our	trail.

48. In The End

(From the Solo Edition of the Secular Hymnal - key unchanged)

Tune: "Assurance" by Phoebe Palmer Knapp, 1873
(traditional hymn: "Blessed Assurance")

Words & Chords: Secretary Michael

1. In__ the end, where__ will__ we be? In__ a vil - la by__ the sea? In__ a
2. So__ let's make this the best it can be, good as a vil - la by__ the sea, good as a

snow - y moun-tain cha - let? On__ an is - land far - a - way? But the sta-
snow - y moun-tain cha - let, good as an is - land far - a - way. Keep-ing our

tis - tics say it ain't so. And the sta - tis - tics say we won't go. And the sta-
neigh - bors free__ from fear, keep-ing our air and wa - ter clear, and our kids

tis - tics make__ it clear: that in the end_____ we will be here.
smil - ing ear__ to ear, 'cuz in the end_____ we will be here.

49. Informed People

(From the Solo Edition of the Secular Hymnal - key lowered from G to F)

Tune: "Helmsley"
(traditional hymn: "Lo He Comes With Clouds Descending")

Words & Chords: Secretary Michael

In - formed_ peo - ple tend to live their lives re - spon - si - bly.
In - formed_ peo - ple tend to un - der-stand di - ver - si - ty.

In - for - ma - tion brings sta - bi - li - ty._____
In - for - ma - tion builds com - mu - ni - ty._____

Jour - nal - ists you teach us. Jour - nal - ists you let us see.

Jour - nal-ists you help_ us live our_ lives re - spon - si - bly.

50. Injustice To You Is Injustice To Me

(From the Solo Edition of the Secular Hymnal - key lowered from G to F)

Tune: "St. Clement" by Clement Cotterill Scholefield, 1874
(traditional hymn: "The Day Thou Gavest Lord Is Ended")

Words & Chords: Secretary Michael

In - jus - tice to you is in - jus - tice to me is the
way that I want my life to be. To
see e - v'ry - bo - dy with e - qua - li - ty, where in -
jus - tice to you is in - jus - tice to me.

51. Intelligence is a Bouquet

(From the Solo Edition of the Secular Hymnal - key unchanged)

Words & Chords: Secretary Michael

Tune: "St. Margaret" by Albert Lister Peace
(traditional hymn: "O Love That Will Not Let Me Go")

In - tel - li - gence is a bou - quet_____ with count - less flow - ers on dis -

play.   In - stead   of look - ing for just   one,_____   may

we   dis - co - ver the in - tel - li - gence in e - v'ry - one.

52. It's Great To Know Some Things By Heart

(From the Solo Edition of the Secular Hymnal - key lowered from Eb to D)

Words & Chords: Secretary Michael

Tune: "Repton" by Charles Hubert Hastings Parry, 1888
(traditional hymn: "Dear Lord and Father of Mankind")

It's great to know_ some_ things by heart and feel that we are smart. Like

3 point 1 4 1 5 9 2 6 5 3 5 8 it's___ great to___

know some things_ by___ heart and feel that we are smart.

This song calculates Pi to 11 decimals.
Pi calculated to 100 decimals is:
3.14159265358979323846264338
32795028841971693993751058
20974944592307816406286
2089986280348253421170679...

53. I've Never Known a Sinner

(From the Solo Edition of the Secular Hymnal - key unchanged)

Words & Chords: Secretary Michael

Tune: "Azmon" by Carl Gotthelf Glaser, 1828
(traditional hymn: "O for a Thousand Tongues to Sing")

Lyrics:

1. I've ne-ver known a sin-ner and I doubt I e-ver will. Al-though I know of those who lie, and those who steal and kill. A cue ball hits a-no-ther ball, which hits a-no-ther still. And none of them re-fuse to move or move of their free will.

2. And so it is with mo-le-cules and neu-rons in the brain. When one will bump a-no-ther one, the next must do the same. I've ne-ver known a sin-ner in the peo-ple I have seen, be-cause I some-how un-der-stand we're in the same ma-chine.

54. Journey Forward

(From the Solo Edition of the Secular Hymnal - key unchanged)

Words & Chords: Secretary Michael

Tune: William Tomer, 1880
(traditional hymn: "God Be With You Till We Meet Again")

1. Jour - ney for - ward, stu - dy e - v'ry - thing. Make the whole world your con - cern.____
2. Jour - ney for - ward lov - ing e - v'ry - one, old and young and the in - firm.____

Learn what - e - ver you can learn.____ We'll be wait - ing____ your re - turn. Your re-
Earn the friends that you can earn.____ We'll be wait - ing____ your re - turn. Your re-

REFRAIN

turn,____ ____ your re - turn,____ we'll be wait - ing your____ re - turn. Your re-

turn,____ ____ your re - turn.____ We'll be wait - ing____ your re - turn.

55. Just Because

(From the Solo Edition of the Secular Hymnal - key lowered from D to C)

Tune: "Monks Gate" (traditional English)
Metric Simplification: Secretary Michael
(traditional hymn: "He Who Would Valiant Be")

Words & Chords: Secretary Michael

Just be-cause it's etched in gold, does - n't mean it's good.
Just be-cause the words_ might rhyme, does - n't mean they're true.

Just be-cause the o - thers do, does - n't mean we should.
Just be-cause we may - be can, does - n't mean we do.

Just be-cause it might be___ old, does - n't mean it's wise.
Just be-cause the wolf might_ cry, does - n't mean it's sad.

Just be-cause it might_ have wings, does - n't mean it flies.
Just be-cause the bird_ might sing, does - n't mean it's glad.

56. Land of Gray

(From the Solo Edition of the Secular Hymnal - key lowered from F to D)

Words & Chords: Secretary Michael

Tune: "Hyfrydol" by Rowland Hugh Prichard, 1830
(traditional hymn: "Love Divine, All Loves Excelling")

1. On our jour - ney let's spend time in the place they call the "Land of Gray".
2. In this mixed - up, mes - sy land, we can learn to love and un - der - stand.

Not quite night, yet not quite day, it's not to - mor - row, yet not to - day.
Not quite wo - man, not quite man, it's not quite Bi - ble yet not Qu - ran.

Not quite left yet not quite right, it's not quite black yet not quite white.
Not quite West, yet not quite East, it's not quite hu - man yet not quite beast.

Not quite here, yet not quite a - way, Let's spend time in the "Land of Gray".
Can't quite leave, yet can't quite stay, here at home in the "Land of Gray".

57. Let's Make a Right

(From the Solo Edition of the Secular Hymnal - key lowered from F to D)

Tune: "Italian Hymn" by Felice de Giardini, 1769
(traditional hymn: "Come Thou Almighty King")

Words & Chords: Secretary Michael

1. Let's make **clean wa - ter** a right. Let's make **clean wa - ter** our fight.
2.   **nu - tri - tion**   **nu - tri - tion**
3.   **health care**   **health care**
4.   **edu - ca - tion**   **edu - ca - tion**
5.   **oppor - tuni - ty**   **oppor - tu - ni - ty**
6.   **shel - ter**   **shel - ter**
7.   **peace**   **peace**

This is our quest: That we will work to bring re - lief from

suf - fer - ing. 'Til we a - chieve this thing, we shall not rest.

58. Let's Ride in our Time Machines

(From the Solo Edition of the Secular Hymnal - key lowered from G to F)

Words & Chords: Secretary Michael

Tune: "Garden" by Charles Austin Miles, 1912
(traditional hymn: "In the Garden")

1. Let's ride in our time__ ma- chines__ in - to fu - tures of__ our dreams.__ And__
2. For those who do not have the means__ to go riding in time__ ma - chines,__ let's__

if we could on-ly look for good in pla - ces ne - ver seen.__ Let's__
bring them a - long and__ teach them our song, and share with them our dreams.__ Let's__

REFRAIN

look out- side as we ride, ride, ride through fields and fields__ of flo - wers, and__

sing our song as we speed a - long at six - ty__ mi -nutes per ho - ur.

59. Let's Start a Big Commotion

(From the Solo Edition of the Secular Hymnal - key lowered from C to A)

Tune: "Thaxted" by Gustaf T. Holst, 1921
(traditional hymn: "I Vow to Thee, My Country")

Words & Chords: Secretary Michael

Let's__ start a big com - mo - tion so e - v'ry - bo - dy knows a -

bout a great in - jus - tice that they can help op - pose. Let's

shake the foun - da - tions, let's shout and bang the drums, be - cause

si - lence is vio - lence if it gets no - thing done. To

end a great in - jus - tice it must__ be ex - posed. So let's

start a big com - mo - tion so e - v'ry - bo - dy knows.

60. Let's Stop Making Weapons

(From the Solo Edition of the Secular Hymnal - key unchanged)

Tune: "Sparrow" by Charles Hutchinson Gabriel, 1905
(traditional hymn: "His Eye Is on the Sparrow")

Words & Chords: Secretary Michael

1. Suf - fer - ing 'round the world, car - nage and so much fear, co - ming from some - thing ug - ly,
2. Con - flicts can be re - solved, and in a heal - ing way. Sim - ply ask a - ny teach - er;

some - thing that we make here. It's not our mo - vies or veg - gies, or cars we proud - ly dis - play,___ or
they do it e - v'ry - day. Or ask the au - to me - cha - nic, the veg - gie far - mer and son, and

a - ny - thing we are ma - king___ in a "Love Thy Neigh - bor" way. We hide it cuz it's
o - thers that we look up to,___ who re - fuse to own a gun. A dif - f'rent way of

REFRAIN

shame - ful,___ but we make them e - v'ry - day. The world can have our mo - vies,___ our veg - gies and our
think - ing,___ but the think - ing must get done. The world...

cars. But let's stop mak - ing wea - pons, 'cuz that's not who we are.

61. Let's Try Something Different

(From the Solo Edition of the Secular Hymnal - key lowered from Bb to A)

Tune: "Evangel" by William Howard Doane, 1867
(traditional hymn: "Tell Me the Old, Old Story")

Words & Chords: Secretary Michael

Let's try some-thing dif - f'rent that we've not tried be - fore. We've
tried and tried__ the__ tried and true, so let's try some - thing__ more.
Let's__ go to dif - f'rent pla - ces and o - pen__ dif - f'rent doors with
dif - f'rent peo - ple and__ points of view that we can - not ig - nore.
Let's try some - thing dif - f'rent. Let's try some - thing dif - f'rent.
Let's try some - thing dif - f'rent. Let's try some - thing more.

62. Long Road

(From the Solo Edition of the Secular Hymnal - key lowered from Am to Gm)

Words & Chords: Secretary Michael

Tune: "Meine Hoffnung Stehet Feste" by J.Neander, 1680
(traditional hymn:"All My Hope On God Is Founded")

Long Road, Long Road, where you take me? Why these prob - lems, why this stress?

Long Road, Long Road, don't for - sake me. We are bound for hap - pi - ness.

Long Road, Long Road, we are bound for hap - pi - ness.

Long Road, Long Road, we will get there, get there yet.

63. Make Just One Brand-New Friend

(From the Solo Edition of the Secular Hymnal - key unchanged)

Words & Chords: Secretary Michael

Tune: "Foundation" by Joseph Funk, 1832
(traditional hymn: "How Firm a Foundation")

Make just one brand new friend who seems dif - f'rent and strange. Make just

one brand new friend, and your whole world will change. Just

one brand new friend who seems dif - f'rent and strange. Make just

one brand new friend and your whole world will change.

64. May We Make Moments of Peace

(From the Solo Edition of the Secular Hymnal - key lowered from C to Bb)

Words & Chords: Secretary Michael

Tune: "Duke Street" by John Hatton, 1793
(traditional hymn: "Jesus Shall Reign, Where'er the Sun")

Bb   **F**   **Eb**   **Bb**

May we make mo - ments of peace and of light,

Dm   **Eb**   **Cm**   **F**

Each lit - tle mo - ment to brigh - ten the night.

Bb   **Gm**   **Eb**   **F**

Mo - ments will lead to more and more that ne - ver cease

Bb   **Gm**   **F⁷**   **Bb**

Un - til the world be - comes a mo - ment of peace.

65. No Cheers For David

(From the Solo Edition of the Secular Hymnal - key lowered from D to C)

Words & Chords: Secretary Michael

Tune: "O Perfect Love" by Joseph Barnby, 1889
(traditional hymn: "O Perfect Love")

| C | G7 | C | E | F |

No cheers for Da - vid, no cheers for Go - li - ath.

| Dm | G7 | C | E | Am | D | G | G7 |

No cheers when "Good Guys" bat - tle with the "Bad".

| C | G7 | C | E | F |

We must for peace - ful re - so - lu - tions cheer,_____

| Dm | G7 | Am | Dm | G7 | C |

so vio - lent vic - to - ries will dis - ap - pear.

66. No Need to Sing the Same Notes

(From the Solo Edition of the Secular Hymnal - key lowered from Ab to G)

Words & Chords: Secretary Michael

Tune: "Wir Pflugen" (We Plow) by Johann A.P.Schulz, 1800
(traditional hymn: "We Plow the Fields and Scatter")

Lyrics:

No need to sing the same notes that sound i - den - ti - c'ly, when

we can all sing dif - f'rent notes that sound in har - mo - ny. The

mu - sic can be ri - cher when there's di - ver - si - ty. So

let's not sing the same notes, let's sing in har - mo - ny.

67. Nonviolence May Take a Long Time

(From the Solo Edition of the Secular Hymnal - key unchanged)

Words & Chords: Secretary Michael

Tune: "Redeemed" by William James Kirkpatrick, 1882
(traditional hymn: "Redeemed")

Non - vio-lence may take a long time, but al - ways is best in the end. Non -

vio-lence may take a long time, so now is the time to be - gin. Be -

gin, be - gin, so now is the time to be - gin. Be -

gin, be - gin, so now is the time to be - gin.

68. Nonviolence Must Be Taught

(From the Solo Edition of the Secular Hymnal - key lowered from Eb to C)

Words & Chords: Secretary Michael

Tune: "All in the April Evening" by Hugh S. Roberton, 1911
(traditional hymn: "All in the April Evening")

Learn - ing to read and learn - ing to write. Such im - por - tant___ skills.

Learn - ing to swim and learn - ing to bike up and down the___ hills.

Learn - ing to tie our shoes and to do the things we ought.

Like all im - por - tant skills, non - vio - lence must be taught.

69. Nothing's Heavy With Lots of Hands

(From the Solo Edition of the Secular Hymnal - key lowered from F to Eb)

Tune: "Hendon" by Henri Abraham Cesar Malan, 1827
(traditional hymn: "Take My Life and Let It Be")

Words & Chords: Secretary Michael

1. No - thing's hea - vy with___ lots of hands shar - ing bur - dens,
2. No - thing's stuck with lots of feet mov - ing 'til the
3. No - thing's hard with lots of minds, not just yours and

shar - ing plans. A - ny - thing that life de - mands, lift - ing, pull - ing,
job's com - plete. Step by step and beat by beat, in the mud or
not just mine. All the peo - ple all com - bined sol - ving pro - blems

yes we can. No - thing's hea - vy with lots of hands.
on the street. No - thing's stuck with lots of feet.
for man - kind. No - things hard with lots of minds.

70. Oh Child Do Not Despair

(From the Solo Edition of the Secular Hymnal - key lowered from F to Eb)

Words & Chords: Secretary Michael

Tune: "St. Thomas" by Aaron Williams (c. 1770)
(traditional hymn: "O Bless the Lord, My Soul")

Chords (first line): Eb Cm Ab Bb Eb Fm Bb

1. Oh child do not de - spair, it's hard to see from there. So
2. And on our shoul - ders__ stand to sur - vey all the land. Then
3. May chil - dren e - v'ry__ where not e - ver know de - spair. May

Chords (second line): Eb Bb Cm Gm Ab Bb Eb

let us lift you way up high so you can see the sky.
look - ing far and look - ing free please tell us what you see.
all find shoul - ders to the sky and all be lif - ted high.

71. Ojalá

(From the Solo Edition of the Secular Hymnal - key lowered from F to D)

Words & Chords: Secretary Michael

Tune: *Katholisches Gesangbuch* (Vienna) 1686
(traditional hymn: "Holy God, We Praise Thy Name")

1. O - ja - lá that luck will come. O - ja - lá for
2. O - ja - lá for life - long health. O - ja - lá for

e - v'ry - one. O - ja - lá for work to do.
need - ed wealth. O - ja - lá for trea - sures won.

REPEATING REFRAIN

O - ja - lá for me and you. But what - e - ver
O - ja - lá for those with none. But what - e - ver

fate may bring, O - ja lá is what we'll sing.
fate may bring, O - ja - lá is what we'll sing.

* *Ohalá* (pronounced: *Oh-ha-LAH*) is the beautiful Spanish word meaning "let us hope"

72. Onward Upward

(From the Solo Edition of the Secular Hymnal - key lowered from D to C)

Words & Chords: Secretary Michael

Tune: "St. Gertrude" by Arthur Seymour Sullivan, 1871
(traditional hymn: "Onward Christian Soldiers")

On - ward, up - ward here we go, off to build new roads. Roads strong and smooth to

car - ry hea - vy loads. Roads to free - dom, roads to peace, peace for e - v'ry - one.

Work- ing, work- ing, work- ing, work- ing, work- ing 'til we're done. On- ward, up-ward here we go,

roads through e - v'ry_ wall. Work- ing for a world, a world that works for all.

73. Open Open Up the Window

(From the Solo Edition of the Secular Hymnal - key unchanged)

Tune: "Austrian Hymn" by Franz Joseph Hayden, 1797
(traditional hymn: "Glorious Things of Thee Are Spoken")

Words & Chords: Secretary Michael

O - pen, o - pen up the win - dow. Let the cur - tains snap in the wind.

O - pen, o - pen up the win - dow. Let the fresh new world come_ in.

May we all_ grow as the winds blow, blow and blow and blow a - gain.

O - pen, o - pen up the win - dow. Let the_ fresh_ new_ world come_ in.

74. Our Garden Full of Flowers

(From the Solo Edition of the Secular Hymnal - key lowered from Am to F#m)

Words & Chords: Secretary Michael

Tune: "Passion Chorale" by Hans Leo Hassler, 1601
(traditional hymn: "O Sacred Head, Now Wounded")

Lyrics underneath the staves:

Line 1 (measures 1–4):
1. Our gar - den full of flow - ers, of veg' - ta - bles__ and greens, of
2. The hates and fears with - in us all want at - ten - tion too. And
3. Our peace we keep it liv - ing by tend - ing to__ its needs, by

Line 2 (measures 5–8):
on - ions and to - ma - toes, of pep - pers and__ of beans. We
e - v'ry time they get it, they do what they__ will do. When
prac - ti - cing non - vio - lence in thought and word__ and deed. Our

Line 3 (measures 9–12):
fer - ti - lize and weed them and wa - ter e - v'ry row. The
hates__ and fears con - trol us and ne - ver want to go, the
peace__ re - quires we care for the peo - ple we don't know. The

Line 4 (measures 13–16):
more__ that we at - tend them, the more that they will grow.
more__ that we at - tend them, the more that they will grow.
more__ that we at - tend them, the more our peace will grow.

75. Pain Can Cause

(From the Solo Edition of the Secular Hymnal - key lowered from D to C)

Tune: "Adelaide" by George Coles Stebbins, 1907
(traditional hymn: "Have Thine Own Way, Lord")

Words & Chords: Secretary Michael

Lyrics:

C   F   C   G   G⁷

1. Pain can cause thoughts that ne - ver re - lax.   Pain can cause
2. Pain can cause breaks in fa - mi - ly ties.   Pain can make

C

tears and de - sper - ate acts.   In - stead of
friend - ships crum - ble and die.   In - stead of

F   C   C⁷   F   C°⁷

judg - ing, we should re - frain.   We can - not
judg - ing, we should re - frain.   We can - not

C   G⁷   C

know_____ a - ny - one's pain.
know_____ a - ny - one's pain.

76. Parents Gone

(From the Solo Edition of the Secular Hymnal - key lowered from D dorian to B dorian)

Tune: "Wondrous Love" from *Southern Harmony*, 1835
(traditional hymn: "What Wondrous Love Is This")

Words & Chords: Secretary Michael

1. If you could see me now, Pa-rents Gone, Pa-rents Gone, if you could see me
2. If you could hear me now, Pa-rents Gone, Pa-rents Gone, if you could hear me
3. If you could hold me now, Pa-rents Gone, Pa-rents Gone, if you could hold me

now, Pa-rents Gone. Would you know whom you see? Would you be proud of
now, Pa-rents Gone. Would you re-ject my song? Or would you sing a-
now, Pa-rents Gone. My love would o-ver-flow, I ne-ver would let

me? If you could see me now, Pa - rents Gone, Pa - rents
long? If you could hear me now, Pa - rents Gone, Pa - rents
go. If you could hold me now, Pa - rents Gone, Pa - rents

Gone, if you could see me now, Pa - rents Gone.
Gone, if you could hear me now, Pa - rents Gone.
Gone, if you could hold me now, Pa - rents Gone.

77. Past Performance is No Guarantee

(From the Solo Edition of the Secular Hymnal - key lowered from E to C)

Tune: "Mannheim" by Friedrich Filitz, 1847
(traditional hymn: "Lead Us Heavenly Father Lead Us")

Words & Chords: Secretary Michael

Past per - for - mance is no guar - an - tee of what our fu - tures hold.

Things we val - ued in our youth might not be val - ued when we're old.

Let's in - vest in - to our fu - tures though there are no guar - an - tees.

Young and old need love and peace so let us all in - vest in these.

(The title [and first line] of this Secular Hymn comes from a common disclaimer that investment companies use: "Past Performance is No Guarantee of Future Results")

78. Peace is Not What I Looked For

(From the Solo Edition of the Secular Hymnal - key lowered from Eb to D)

Words & Chords: Secretary Michael

Tune: Charles Crozat Converse, 1868
(traditional hymn: "What a Friend We Have In Jesus")

D ... **G** ... **D** ... **A**

Peace is not___ what I looked for. Peace is not___ what I got.

D ... **G** ... **D** ... **A⁷** ... **D**

Looked to give___ some-one trou - bles. Trou - bles now___ I've a lot.

A ... **D** ... **G** ... **Em** ... **A**

If a flow - er is - n't cared for, it will die___ in its pot.

D ... **G** ... **D** ... **A⁷** ... **D**

Peace is not___ what I looked for. Peace is not___ what I got.

79. Peace Like a River

(From the Solo Edition of the Secular Hymnal - key lowered from G to F)

(Substitute this rhythm for all
similar 4th-verse occurrences)

Peace, Love and Joy like a

Tune and Words: traditional American
Adapted by Secretary Michael
(traditional hymn: "I've Got Peace Like a River")

1. I've got PEACE LIKE A RI - VER, I've got PEACE LIKE A RI - VER, I've got
2. (I've got) LOVE LIKE AN O - CEAN, I've got LOVE LIKE AN O - CEAN,
3. (I've got) JOY LIKE A FOUN - TAIN, I've got JOY LIKE A FOUN - TAIN,
4. (I've got) [see insert] A RI - VER, I've got [see insert] A RI - VER,

(peace like a ri - ver) in my soul. I've got

(peace like a ri - ver), I've got (peace like a ri - ver), I've got

(peace like a ri - ver) in my soul._____ I've got soul._____

80. People Are More

(From the Solo Edition of the Secular Hymnal - key lowered from Dm to Bm)

Words & Chords: Secretary Michael

Tune: "Aberystwyth" by Joseph Parry, 1879
(traditional hymn: "Jesus Lover Of My Soul")

Peo - ple are more_ than the worst they've done. More than "fe - lon", more than "ex - con".

Peo - ple are more_ than the worst they've done. More than of - fen - der, more than scum.

More than fail - ure, more than de - feat. More than li - ar, more than cheat.

E - ven a kil - ler with a gun. Peo - ple are more_ than the worst they've done.

81. People We Need to Meet

(From the Solo Edition of the Secular Hymnal - key lowered from D to C)

Words & Chords: Secretary Michael

Tune: Silesian Folk Song
(traditional hymn: "Fairest Lord Jesus")

| C | G⁷ | C | G⁷ | C |

Peo - ple we need to meet. Jour - neys we must com - plete.

| Am | Em | Dm | F | G |

Those we once hid are now those we must seek.

| C | A | Dm | G | C |

No more are we a - fraid. No more will we e - vade. The

| Am | A⁷ | F | G⁷ | C |

time is now, let peace be made.

82. People Will Change

(From the Solo Edition of the Secular Hymnal - key lowered from F to Eb)

Words & Chords: Secretary Michael

Tune: "Lobe Den Herren" by Joachim Neander, 1685
(traditional hymn: "Praise to the Lord")

1. Peo - ple will change when put in dif - frent si - tu - a - tions.
2. Peo - ple will change when suf - fring dif - frent de - pri - va - tions.

Peo - ple will change when work - ing dif - frent oc - cu - pa - tions.
Peo - ple will change when tak - ing dif - frent me - di - ca - tions.

Change can cause strife, but it is part___ of life.

So we must make a - dap - ta - tions.

83. Relieving Suffering

(From the Solo Edition of the Secular Hymnal - key lowered from G to F)

Tune: "Need" by Robert Lowry, 1872
(traditional hymn: "I Need Thee Every Hour")

Words & Chords: Secretary Michael

Re - liev - ing Suf - fer - ing. It's all I care to sing. It's

all I know that's true. It's all I care to do. If

I can bring re - lief, I'm liv - ing my be - lief. It's

all I care to sing: Re - liev - ing Suf - fer - ing.

84. Rise and Shine

(From the Solo Edition of the Secular Hymnal - key lowered from G to F)

Words & Chords: Secretary Michael

Tune: "Holy Manna" by William Moore, 1825
(traditional hymn: "Brethren, We Have Met to Worship")

1. Rise and Shine, a new day's dawn- ing, chance to make a bet- ter day.
2. Rise and Shine, the page is turn- ing, turn- ing in- to de - sti - ny.

Rise and Shine, get up, stop yawn- ing, chance to go a dif - f'rent way.
Rise and Shine, the book is clos- ing, clos- ing in - to his - to - ry.

One more chance to join the tus - sle. One more chance be - fore the night.
No more time for nur - sing sor - row. No more time to wish and whine.

Chance to lend my mind and mu - scle. Chance to fi - n'ly get things right.
Time is now and not to - mor - row. Time is now to Rise and Shine.

85. Seen, Heard and Understood

(From the Solo Edition of the Secular Hymnal - key lowered from Eb to D)

Tune: "Bethany" by Lowell Mason, 1856
(traditional hymn: "Nearer My God, To Thee")

Words & Chords: Secretary Michael

"Seen, Heard and Un - der stood" If but we could.

"Seen, Heard and Un - der- stood" All_____ would be good.

Such ba - sic hu - man needs. Such lov - ing hu - man deeds.

"Seen, Heard and Un - der- stood" If_____ but we could.

86. Skating, Skating

(From the Solo Edition of the Secular Hymnal - key unchanged)

Words & Chords: Secretary Michael

Tune: "Westminster Abbey" by Henry Purcell, c.1680
(traditional hymn: "Christ is Made the Sure Foundation")

Lyrics:

Skat - ing, skat - ing all a-round, a time will come__ when we fall down.

Time will come when all seems lost, a time will come__ of pain - ful cost.

Pay tu - i - tion, then re - turn, for fall - ing down is how we learn.

87. So Many Ways

(From the Solo Edition of the Secular Hymnal - key lowered from D to C)

Tune: "Billing" by Sir Richard Runciman Terry, 1912
(traditional hymn: "Praise to the Holiest in the Height")

Words & Chords: Secretary Michael

So ma - ny ways to live our lives and
so ma - ny notes to sing. Let's
choose our notes and live_____ our lives re -
liev - - ing suf - - fer - ing.

88. Some Are Young, Some Old

(From the Solo Edition of the Secular Hymnal - key lowered from F to D)

Words & Chords: Secretary Michael

Tune: "Anchor" by William James Kirkpatrick, 1882
(traditional hymn: "Will Your Anchor Hold?")

Some are young, some old, some are shy, some bold. Some are weak, some strong, some are right, some wrong. Some are bound, some free, some are blind, some see. But to-ge-ther we're a com-mu-ni-ty. We stand to-ge-ther, we stand by choice, though each of us has a dif-frent voice. So let's try to sing in har-mo-ny, 'cuz to-ge-ther we're a com-mu-ni-ty.

89. Someday When Guns Are Gone

(From the Solo Edition of the Secular Hymnal - key lowered from Eb to D)

Tune: "Dennis" by Johann Georg Nageli
(traditional hymn: "Blest Be the Tie That Binds")

Words & Chords: Secretary Michael

Some - day___ when guns___ are gone and ci - vi - li - za - tion moves on, they'll look back in dread at our bul - lets of lead and our mil - lions and mil - lions of dead.

90. Someone Should

(From the Solo Edition of the Secular Hymnal - key unchanged)

Tune: "Cwm Rhondda" by John Hughes, 1907
(traditional hymn: "Guide Me, O Thou Great Jehovah")

Words & Chords: Secretary Michael

1. Some - one should clean up__ this__ mess!__ (Hey, I am a some - one too!)
2. Some - one should re - spect__ our__ rules!__ (Hey, I am a some - one too!)

Some - one should stand up,__ say__ "Yes!"__ (Hey, I am a____
Some - one should sup - port__ our__ schools!__ (Hey, I am a____

some - one too!) All these things that no - one's do - ing,
some - one too!) All these things that no - one's do - ing,

some - one needs_ to__ do (Hey, I am__ a__ some - one too!)
some - one needs_ to__ do (Hey, I am__ a__ some - one too!)

91. Spent Our Treasure

(From the Solo Edition of the Secular Hymnal - key lowered from Eb to D)

Words & Chords: Secretary Michael

Tune: "Were You There?" (traditional African-American spiritual)
(traditional hymn: "Were You There When They Crucified My Lord?")

Spent our trea - sure on U two thir - ty five. *(man alive!)* Spent our
Spent our trea - sure on brand new war ma - chines. *(how obscene!)* Spent our

trea - sure on U two thir - ty five. *(man alive!)*
trea - sure on brand new war ma - chines. *(how obscene!)*

Did we de - cide that schools would all sur - vive and thrive, thrive,
Was it our dream the help-less would get the means, the means, means,

thrive?_____ No. We spent it on U two thir - ty five. *(man alive!)*
means?_____ No. We spent it on brand new war ma chines. *(how obscene!)*

(Explanation: U-235 is bomb-grade uranium which is refined from common uranium through expensive processing)

92. Standing At Bat

(From the Solo Edition of the Secular Hymnal - key lowered from F to D)

Words & Chords: Secretary Michael

Tune: "Hamburg" by Lowell Mason, 1824
(traditional hymn: "When I Survey the Wondrous Cross")

D	Bm	G	D

1. Stand - ing at bat as the teams look at me.
2. Peo - ple from here say to fight for the "red".
3. Why in the world should I fight for a team?

Bm	G	Em	A

Should I de - li - ver what they want to see?
Peo - ple from there shout out "yel - low" in - stead.
If we want peace, we must stand in be - tween.

D	Bm	G	D

What will it mean when it's o - ver and done?
Now as I won - der if a - ny - thing's true,
If we want peace, then it's peace we must be.

Bm	G	A⁷	D

Ump looks at me and shouts "Strike One!"
Ump looks at me and shouts "Strike Two!"
I look at Ump and I say "Strike Three."

93. Step by Step

(From the Solo Edition of the Secular Hymnal - key unchanged)

Words & Chords: Secretary Michael

Tune: "China" by William Batchelder Bradbury, 1862
(traditional hymn: "Jesus Loves Me, This I Know")

Step by step we march a - long, al - ways right and ne - ver wrong.

Step by step and straight a - head, 'til we learn to dance in - stead.

Slide, kick and hip - hop. Slide, kick and hip - hop.

Slide, kick and hip - hop. Let's learn to dance in - stead.

94. Storms Will Come

(From the Solo Edition of the Secular Hymnal - key lowered from A to G)

Words & Chords: Secretary Michael

Tune: "St. Helen" by Sir George C Martin, 1889
(traditional hymn: "Lord Enthroned in Heavenly Splendor")

Storms will come and storms will go,___ caus - ing da - mage as they blow.

Blow and blow un - til they're done,___ storms will vi - sit e - v'ry - one.

Storms will come, but come what may,___ storms will al - ways go a - way.

95. Striving To Be

(From the Solo Edition of the Secular Hymnal - key lowered from G to D)

Words & Chords: Secretary Michael

Tune: "Pentecost" by William Boyd, 1868
(traditional hymn: "Fight the Good Fight")

Striv - ing to be some - one who's rich,

work - ing so hard to scratch that itch.

But there's an itch that we need more:

Striv - ing to be some - one who's poor.

PD *All works by Secretary Michael have been placed in the Public Domain. They may be freely copied and performed.*

96. Swapping Shoes

(From the Solo Edition of the Secular Hymnal - key lowered from G to F)

Words & Chords: Secretary Michael

Tune: "Dix" by Conrad Kocher, 1838
(traditional hymn: "For the Beauty of the Earth")

| F | Dm | B♭ | F | B♭ | Dm | C | F |

Swap - ping__ shoes with those we blame, shows that we would do the same.

| F | Dm | B♭ | F | B♭ | Dm | C | F |

Swap - ping__ shoes with those we fear, we'd be there and they'd be here.

| F | Dm | C | F | B♭ | Dm | C⁷ | F |

Swap - ping shoes, a use - ful game, shows how much we're all the same.

97. Tall Oaks From Little Acorns Grow

(From the Solo Edition of the Secular Hymnal - key lowered from D to C)

Tune: "St. Columba" (traditional Irish melody)
(traditional hymn: "The King of Love My Shepherd Is")

Words & Chords: Secretary Michael

Lyrics:

Tall oaks from little acorns grow. They grow and grow and grow oh. And friend-ships start from just "hel-lo". Hel-lo, hel-lo, hel-lo oh.

98. The Greatest Walk

(From the Solo Edition of the Secular Hymnal - key lowered from D to C)

Words & Chords: Secretary Michael

Tune: Sir Hubert Parry, 1916
(traditional hymn: "Jerusalem")

The great-est walk we'll e - ver take is the jour-ney we must make. Where e - v'ry

wo - man, e - v'ry man must fi - gure out a way we can walk through this

life to - ge - ther, no mat - ter what the wea - ther, no mat - ter

what the mood, what the talk, put down our cru - tches and walk.

99. The Many Truths

(From the Solo Edition of the Secular Hymnal - key lowered from F to D)

Words & Chords: Secretary Michael

Tune: *Finlandia* by Jean Sibelius, 1899
(traditional hymn: "Be Still My Soul")

The ma - ny truths that peo - ple car - ry with them. The ma - ny truths that help them get through life. And though their truths may dif - fer from our own,— may we ac - cept and ne - ver cause them strife. May we be strong and guard them as they car -ry the ma - ny truths that help them get through life.

100. The Only Path to Peace is Peace

(From the Solo Edition of the Secular Hymnal - key lowered from C to A)

Words & Chords: Secretary Michael

Tune: "St. Anne" by William Croft, 1708
(traditional hymn: "Our God Our Help in Ages Past")

The on-ly path to peace is peace so don't be led a-stray by
those who love their bombs and guns and shout out "U. S. A". Let's
not re-peat the same mis-takes that we made yes-ter-day. The
on-ly path to peace is peace, so peace must be our way.

101. Them Over There

(From the Solo Edition of the Secular Hymnal - key lowered from D to C)

Words & Chords: Secretary Michael

Tune: Lasst Uns Erfreuen (pre-1623)
(traditional hymn: "All Creatures Of Our God and King")

1. Them o - ver there who don't have names. Them o - ver there who seem the same.
2. We o - ver here can make a change. We can go there and learn their names.

Seem the same.___ Don't have names.___ Them o - ver there, the old and frail.
Make a change.___ Learn their names.___ Names for the old and for the frail.

Them o - ver there, the young in jail. Them with can - cer and no hair.___
Names for the lost and those in jail. If we care___ we must dare___

Schi - zo - phre - nics in de - spair.___ Them___ there.___
learn their names 'til there's no "them" and there's no "there".___

102. There are Times

(From the Solo Edition of the Secular Hymnal - key unchanged)

Words & Chords: Secretary Michael

Tune: "All To Christ" by John Thomas Grape, 1868
(traditional hymn: "Jesus Paid It All")

C   **Am**   **G**   **C**

1. There are times I want to stop, and times I want to go. But I
2. There are times when I am fast, and times when I am slow. But I
3. There are times when I am high, and times when I am low. But I

5   **Am**   **F**   **G**   **C**

al - ways want to be the___ per - son that I know.
al - ways want to be the___ per - son that I know.
al - ways want to be the___ per - son that I know.

9 **C**   **Am**   **C**   **G**

Times I want to stop. Times I want to go.
Times when I am fast. Times when I am slow.
Times when I am high. Times when I am low.

13 **C**   **F** **F#°7**   **G7**   **C**

But I al - ways want to be the per - son that I know.
But I al - ways want to be the per - son that I know.
But I al - ways want to be the per - son that I know.

103. There is a Game

(From the Solo Edition of the Secular Hymnal - key lowered from G to F)

Words & Chords: Secretary Michael

Tune: "Bring Them In" by William Augustine Ogden, 1885
(traditional hymn: "Bring Them In")

1. There is a game that hor- mones play: They make us fools, then go a - way.
2. An - ger and shout - ing we will see; Dif - f'rent per - so - na - li - ty.

Leav - ing us with a price to pay 'til they come back a - no - ther day.
Oh those ras - cals have such fun mak - ing fools of e - v'ry one.

REFRAIN

Ha - ha - ha! Boo - hoo - hoo! Oh the things that hor- mones do!

Ha - ha - ha! Boo - hoo - hoo! You to me and me to you!

104. There is a Rule of Thumb

(From the Solo Edition of the Secular Hymnal - key lowered from D to C)

Words & Chords: Secretary Michael

Tune: "Diademata" by George J. Elvey, 1868
(traditional hymn: "Crown Him With Many Crowns")

Verse lyrics:

C	Am	F	Em	F	G
1. There is a Rule of Thumb that what will come will come. We'll
2. There is a guar - an - tee that what will be will be. We'll

| C | Am | D⁷ | Em | C | D⁷ | G |
get to where we've got to get and come from where we're from. No
miss the things that we will miss and see what we will see. The

| C | C⁷ | F | D | D⁷ | G |
need for feel - ing pride. No need for feel - ing glum. Let's
do - ing has been done. The end - ing has be - gun. Let's

| Am | F | Dm⁷ | Am | Dm⁷ | G⁷ | C |
side by side en - joy the ride for what will come will come.
side by side en - joy the ride for what will come will come.

105. There is an Empty Box

(From the Solo Edition of the Secular Hymnal - key lowered from D to C)

Tune: "Aurelia" by Samuel Sebastian Wesley, 1864
(traditional hymn: "The Church's One Foundation")

Words & Chords: Secretary Michael

Lyrics:

There is an emp-ty box___ that some would throw a-way. But
o-thers find great beau-ty in-side it e-v'ry day. Although we may not see it, let's all of us a-gree: What
peo-ple see as beau-ty must be al-lowed to be.

106. There is Something Wrong

(From the Solo Edition of the Secular Hymnal - key lowered from Ab to G)

Words & Chords: Secretary Michael

Tune: "The Old Rugged Cross" by George Bennard, 1913
(traditional hymn: "The Old Rugged Cross")

There is some thing wrong if we cheer_ a-long when the peo-ple called "bad"_ are slain____ on a

ci - ne-ma screen or a real - life scene, as if we were in some kind of game.____ A-

game where their death is a plus,____ and a - no - ther point_ for us.____ But if

we are to be____ hu - mane,____ we must get our-selves out of this game.

107. There's a Better Way

(From the Solo Edition of the Secular Hymnal - key unchanged)

Words & Chords: Secretary Michael

Tune: "Blessed Name" (an American camp meeting melody)
(traditional hymn: "Blessed Be the Name")

1. When lea-ders say that vio-lence is the way, there are al-ways those who shout "hoo-ray!" And
2. When lea-ders say that guns will save the day, there are al-ways those who shout "hoo-ray!" And

then, hel - lo, the vio-lence starts to grow. We are stuck with fear and with dis - may.
then, hel - lo, the shoot-ings start to grow. We are stuck with fear and with dis - may.

REFRAIN

There's a bet - ter way! There's a bet - ter way! Peace has al ways been a bet - ter way! No

mat-ter what they say, there's a bet - ter way! Peace has al-ways been a bet - ter way!

(Helpful Hint: there are 5 dotted eighth notes - and they only occur with the word "better")

108. There's a Road Between Our Lands

(From the Solo Edition of the Secular Hymnal - key lowered from G to F)

Tune: "Royal Oak" (a 17th century English melody)
(traditional hymn: "All Things Bright and Beautiful")

Words & Chords: Secretary Michael

There's a road be - tween our__ lands where we can al - ways__ go to

walk to - ge - ther peace - ful - ly and say things from our__ soul. It's

not too hot, it's__ not too cold, it's not__ too left__ or right. Let's__

stay a pair on this road we share and__ ne - ver, ne - ver__ fight.

109. There's Claim Number One

(From the Solo Edition of the Secular Hymnal - key lowered from Eb to D)

Tune: "Revive Us Again" by John Jenkins Husband, c.1815
(traditional hymn: "Revive Us Again")

Words & Chords: Secretary Michael

There's claim num-ber one, and claim num-ber two, and though in-com-pa-ti-ble, both claims are true. With a life-time of claims and their op-po-sites too, seems the best we can do is the best we can do.

110. There's More Than One Way

(From the Solo Edition of the Secular Hymnal - key lowered from G to F)

Words & Chords: Secretary Michael

Tune: "Hanover" by William Croft, 1708
(traditional hymn: "Ye Servants of God")

F   Dm   B♭ C⁷ F

There's more than one way to see what we see. There's

5 Dm   Am   G⁷   C

more than one way to be what____ we be. So

9 Dm   B♭   F   C

when peo - ple have some - thing dif - f'rent to say, let's

13 B♭   C   Gm C F

give them some room 'cuz there's more than one way.

111. Things Are The Way They Are

(From the Solo Edition of the Secular Hymnal - key lowered from D to C)

Tune: "Nun Danket" by Johann Crueger, 1647
(traditional hymn: "Now Thank We All Our God")

Words & Chords: Secretary Michael

Things are the way they are, and not the way they're not._____ Things

go the way they go, and stop the way they stop._____ Un -

til we make the change, it should_ not be for - got: Things

are the way they are, and not the way they're not.

112. This Day, This Day

(From the Solo Edition of the Secular Hymnal - key lowered from F to Eb)

Words & Chords: Secretary Michael

Tune: "Sine Nomine" by Ralph Vaughan Williams, 1906
(traditional hymn: "For All the Saints")

Cm   **A♭**   **B♭7**   **E♭**

This day, this day, I know I'll find a way.

B♭   **F**   **Gm**   **Cm**   **F7**   **B♭**

Let come what may, I'll make it through this day. To -

E♭   **Cm**   **Gm**   **A♭**   **Fm7**   **B♭**   **Gm**

mor - row's fate is not yet on my plate. But

A♭   **Gm**   **Cm**   **A♭**   **Fm**   **B♭7**   **E♭**

come what may, I'll make it through this day.

113. Tick-Tock

(From the Solo Edition of the Secular Hymnal - key lowered from Bb to G)

Words & Chords: Secretary Michael

Tune: "Regent Square" by Henry Thomas Smart, 1867
(traditional hymn: "Angels From the Realms of Glory")

G

Tick - Tock, Tick - Tock   let   it chime 'cuz   time   is   now   a   friend   of   mine.
Tick - Tock, Tick - Tock   no   more need   to   wor - ry   o - ver   things   like   speed.

G   Em   A   A⁷   D   D⁷

Tick - Tock, Tick - Tock   let   it pass, there   ain't   no   slow   and there ain't   no   fast.
Tick - Tock, Tick - Tock   come   my fate,   it   won't   be   ear - ly   and won't   be   late.

D⁷   G   Em   C   D⁷   G

No   more pres - sure,   life   is   fine 'cuz   time   is   now   a   friend   of   mine.
I   will live what   I'm   a - bout   un - til   my   Tick - Tock   time   runs   out.

114. 'Tis a Gift

(From the Solo Edition of the Secular Hymnal - key lowered from F to Eb)

Chords: Secretary Michael

Tune and Words: "Simple Gifts" by Joseph Bracket, 1848
(traditional hymn: "Simple Gifts")

'Tis a gift to be sim-ple, 'tis a gift to be free, 'tis a gift to come down where I ought to be. And

when I am in the place just right, I will be in the val-ley of love and de-light.

When true sim-pli-ci-ty is gained, to bow and to bend I will not be a-shamed. To

turn, to turn will be my de-light, 'til by turn-ing, turn-ing I come 'round right.

115. To Find a Place

(From the Solo Edition of the Secular Hymnal - key lowered from C to Bb)

Words & Chords: Secretary Michael

Tune: "Crucifer" by Sydney Hugo Nicholson, 1916
(traditional hymn: "Lift High the Cross")

REFRAIN

To find a place where they ac - cept my face and
where they let_____ me run_____ an e - ven race.

VERSES

1. Run - ning and run - ning, as a re - fu - gee, I'm
2. Just out of pri - son, try - ing to ad - vance. I'm
3. Once I was mar - ried, now I am a - lone. I'm

run - ning and run - ning, run - ning to be free.
hop - ing and hop - ing for a se - cond chance.
search - ing and search - ing for a place called "home".

116. To Live Our Lives Addiction-Free

(From the Solo Edition of the Secular Hymnal - key lowered from Bb to A)

Words & Chords: Secretary Michael

Tune: "Deus Tuorum Militum", 1753
(traditional hymn: "Bless Thou the Gifts")

Lyrics:

To live our lives ad - dic - tion free. To live our lives with clar - i - ty. Pro - tect our brains so you and me can live the way we're meant to be.

117. To Make the World a Better Place

(From the Solo Edition of the Secular Hymnal - key lowered from D to C)

Tune: "Horsley" by William Horsley, 1830
(traditional hymn: "There Is a Green Hill Far Away")

Words & Chords: Secretary Michael

To make the world a bet - ter___ place, a splen - did thing to do is

take a chance and hire some - one who's dif - fer - ent than you. A

dif - frent skin or dif - frent___ faith or dif - frent point of view. Just___

take a chance and hire some - one who's dif - fer - ent than you.

118. To Soldiers Lost

(From the Solo Edition of the Secular Hymnal - key lowered from Gm to Em)

Words & Chords: Secretary Michael

Tune: "St. Patrick's Breastplate" (traditional Irish)
(traditional hymn: "I Bind Unto Myself Today")

To sol - diers lost in the mad-ness of__ war,__ no mat-ter if this side or that side they are. Our

sol - diers have pro-blems we must ad - dress 'cuz__ we have put__ them in - to this mess. Re-

cruit the young at__ a - ny cost, then call them "he - roes", no won-der they're lost! To

shoot and kill__ o-thers they're du - ty bound. We've lost our__ sol - diers, we must get them found.

119. To Those Who Came Before

(From the Solo Edition of the Secular Hymnal - key lowered from D to C)

Words & Chords: Secretary Michael

Tune: "Down Ampney" by Ralph Vaughan Williams, 1906
(traditional hymn: "Come Down O Love Divine")

To those who came be - fore, and all the work they

bore, we thank you as we stand on your floor.

What now should we get done? What floor have we be -

gun to hold our chil - dren in a world yet to come?

120. Today is My Day

(From the Solo Edition of the Secular Hymnal - key lowered from Eb to C)

Tune: "Trust and Obey" by Daniel Brink Towner, c.1887
Meter changes made by Secretary Michael
(traditional hymn: "Trust and Obey")

Words & Chords: Secretary Michael

"To - day is my day! To - day is my day!" I

sing this to keep a - way sor - row._____ "To -

-day is my day! To - day is my day!" May I

sing it a - gain____ to - mor - row._____

This day I might fin - 'ly get things____ right. But

come__ what may,_____ "To - day is my day!"

121. Today's the Day

(From the Solo Edition of the Secular Hymnal - key lowered from C to Bb)

Words & Chords: Secretary Michael

Tune: "Darwall's 148th" by John Darwall, 1770
(traditional hymn: "Rejoice, the Lord Is King")

Bb	F	Gm	Eb	Cm	F7

To - day's the day at last! I'm chang - ing from my past! I

Bb	Gm	C	C7	F	C7	F

am re - solved I will e - volve, and I'll stand fast! I've

Eb	F7	Gm	Eb	Cm	Cm7	Eb	F	Bb

found my way! It's here at last, good - bye my past, to - day's the day!

122. Together For So Long

(From the Solo Edition of the Secular Hymnal - key lowered from G to F)

Words & Chords: Secretary Michael

Tune: "Lenox" by Lewis Edson, 1782
(traditional hymn: "Arise, My Soul, Arise!")

Line 1 (F, C, Dm, C, F, C):
1. To - ge-ther for so long, but sel - dom do we fight. The o- thers want to know what
2. With fa - mi - ly and friends, or stran-gers met to - day, at home or work or school, things

Line 2 (m. 7 — Dm, C, F, F, B♭, C, Dm):
we are do-ing right. We talk and lis - ten, talk and lis - ten, talk and lis - ten day and night and
al - ways go o - kay. We talk and lis - ten, talk and lis - ten, talk and lis - ten day and night and

Line 3 (m. 13 — B♭, C, C⁷, F, B♭):
that is how we keep things right. We talk and lis - ten, talk and lis - ten,
that is how we keep things right. We talk and lis - ten, talk and lis - ten,

Line 4 (m. 18 — C, Dm, B♭, C, C⁷, F):
talk and lis - ten day and night, and that is how we keep things right.
talk and lis - ten day and night, and that is how we keep things right.

123. T'wards a World That Has No Guns

(From the Solo Edition of the Secular Hymnal - key unchanged)

Words & Chords: Secretary Michael

Tune: from Ludwig van Beethoven's Ninth Symphony, 1824
(traditional hymn: "Joyful, Joyful, We Adore Thee")

T'wards a world that has no guns, where peace is shared by e - v'ry-one.

Let us take a - no - ther step that gets us clo - ser, clo - ser yet.

T'wards a world that's free from fear, where guns are gone and peace is here.

Let us take a - no - ther step that gets us clo - ser, clo - ser yet.

124. Trusting You, Trusting Me

(From the Solo Edition of the Secular Hymnal - key lowered from C to Bb)

Words & Chords: Secretary Michael

Tune: Largo from the "New World Symphony" by Antonin Dvorak, 1893
(popularly known as: "Going Home")

Bb   **Gm**   **Cm⁷**   **F⁷**

Trust - ing you,   trust - ing me.   Trust - ing is the key.

Bb   **D⁷**   **Gm**   **Cm⁷**   **F⁷**   **Bb**

Must be trust.   With - out trust,   no - thing else can be.

Eb   **Dm**   **Eb**   **Dm**   **Eb**

When it's found,   trust un - bound,   all our dreams come true.

Eb   **Dm**   **Eb**   **Eb**   **Dm**   **Eb**

You and me,   fa - mi - ly,   e - v'ry - thing we do.

Bb   **Gm**   **Cm⁷**   **F⁷**

When it's lost,   such a cost,   dreams turn in - to dust.

Bb   **F**   **Gm**   **Dm**   **Cm⁷**   **F⁷**   **Bb**

So my friend,   in the end,   all there is, is trust.

Cm⁷   **F⁷**   **Bb**   **Cm⁷**   **F⁷**   **Bb**

All there is, is trust.   All there is, is trust.

125. Ultimately We May Not Have Free Will

(From the Solo Edition of the Secular Hymnal - key lowered from Em to Dm)

Words & Chords: Secretary Michael

Tune: "Noël Nouvelet" (an old French melody)

Verse 1:
1. Ul - ti - mate - ly we may not have free will.
We may just be peb - bles roll - ing down a hill.
Tum - bling and bounc - ing in a ran - dom race
'til we reach the end with each in a dif - f'rent place.

Verse 2:
2. Ul - ti - mate - ly we may not have free will.
Yet we still blame o - thers for their good and ill.
We still keep pris - 'ners locked up in a cage.
And we still put he - roes high up on a stage.

126. Unconscious Bias

(From the Solo Edition of the Secular Hymnal - key lowered from Em to Dm)

Words & Chords: Secretary Michael

Tune: "Ebenezer" by Thomas John Williams, 1890
(traditional hymn: "Singing Songs of Expectation")

Un - con-scious bi - as, it poi-sons all of us. Al - ways un fair__ but al - ways there.

What can_ we do to keep it__from me and you? What can_ we say__ to keep it a - way?

Say "How do you do?" and meet some-one new, for bi - as__can't win where know ledge has been.

Un - con-scious bi - as, it poi-sons all of us. Al - ways un fair__ but al - ways there.

127. Unless There's No-One Watching

(From the Solo Edition of the Secular Hymnal - key lowered from F to Eb)

Words & Chords: Secretary Michael

Tune: "Endless Song" by Robert Lowry, 1860
(traditional hymn: "How Can I Keep From Singing")

1. I use a spoon to eat my soup un-less there's no-one watch-ing. I
2. I on-ly take one piece of pie un-less there's no-one watch-ing. I

mind my bus-'ness and ne-ver snoop un-less there's no-one watch-ing. I
try to smile and ne-ver cry un-less there's no-one watch-ing. But

wash my hands so care-ful-ly un-less there's no-one watch-ing. I
if there's com-fort I could bring to ease some-bo-dy's suf-f'ring, I

bow my head so___ pi-ous-ly un-less there's no-one watch-ing.
know that I will___ do the right thing, 'cuz I'll be the one who's watch-ing.

128. Wake, Awake

(From the Solo Edition of the Secular Hymnal - key lowered from C to A)

Words & Chords: Secretary Michael

Tune: "Wachet Auf" by Philipp Nicholai, 1599
(traditional hymn: "Wake, Awake For Night Is Flying")

1. Wake, a - wake the night is end - ing! There's some - thing com - ing,
2. Wake, a - wake the veil is lift - ing, with all these won - ders

some - thing big and bright! The world has beau - ty in its light.
com - ing in - to sight! Good day to day, good

night to night. In all e - ter - ni - ty, we have the chance to

see! The chance to see! Get up, get up, let's

use our sight! The world has beau - ty in its light.

(Note: the time signature changes in measures 9 and 14 were added to avoid the fermatas of the traditional version)

129. Walking in Someone's Shoes

(From the Solo Edition of the Secular Hymnal - key lowered from Eb to D)

Words & Chords: Secretary Michael

Tune: Silesian Melody
(traditional hymn: "O God Of Loveliness")

D · **A7** · **D** · **A7** · **D**
Walk - ing in some-one's shoes, some - one with dif - f'rent views.

F#m · **Em** · **Em7** · **A**
Man, wo - man, old or young it does - n't mat - ter whose.

D · **B** · **Em** · **A** · **A#o7** · **Bm**
Walk un - til bit by bit, their shoes be - gin to fit.

D · **F#m** · **G** · **D** · **A7** · **D**
A lov - ing thing to do, to walk in some - one's shoes.

130. We Are People, Plastic People

(From the Solo Edition of the Secular Hymnal - key lowered from C to Bb)

Words & Chords: Secretary Michael

Tune: "Angel Voices" by Edwin G. Monk, 1861
(traditional hymn: "Angel Voices Ever Singing")

Bb   F   Bb   Dm   Gm   Eb   F

We are peo - ple, plas - tic peo - ple, cast from mold to mold.
We are peo - ple, plas - tic peo - ple, cast from die to die.

Bb   Gm   C⁷   F   Gm   C⁷   F

Molds of coun - try, school and work - place all a - cross the globe.
Some dies give us great suc - cess, while some don't e - ven try.

Dm   G⁷   Cm   F⁷   Bb   Gm   Cm⁷   F⁷   Bb

Some molds make us strong and heal - thy, o - thers leave us torn and old.
If we are to change as peo - ple we will have to change the dies.

131. We Are Searching

(From the Solo Edition of the Secular Hymnal - key lowered from C to A)

Words & Chords: Secretary Michael

Tune: "Wondrous Story" by Peter Philip Bilhorn, 1886
(traditional hymn: "I Will Sing the Wondrous Story")

1. We are search - ing for the an - swer, search-ing each and e - v'ry spot. We are
2. We are search - ing for the an - swer, search-ing here and search-ing there. We are

search - ing for the an - swer to a que - stion we for - got. For__ the
search - ing for the an - swer to a que - stion we don't care. For__ the

REFRAIN

joy_____ is in the search - ing far and wide,_____ and up and down. For__ the

joy_____ is in the search - ing for what - e - ver might be found.

132. We Can Be Tolerant

(From the Solo Edition of the Secular Hymnal - key unchanged)

Tune: "Slane" (traditional Irish)
(traditional hymn: "Be Thou My Vision")

Words & Chords: Secretary Michael

| D | Bm | G | A | D |

1. We can be to-ler-ant of dif - fer - ent views,
2. We can be to-ler-ant of dif - fer - ent wealth,

| Em | F#m | G | A(sus4) | A |

dif - frent re - li - gions and dif - frent I - Q's.
dif - fer - ent gen - ders and dif - fer - ent health.

| G | A7 | D | G |

We can___ be___ to - ler - ant of to - ler - ant ones. But
We can___ be___ to - ler - ant of a to - ler - ant lot. But

| D | Bm | G | D |

can we be to - ler - ant of bi - gots with guns?
can we be to - ler - ant of those who are not?

133. We Can Get Things To Happen

(From the Solo Edition of the Secular Hymnal - key unchanged)

Tune: traditional African-American spiritual
(traditional hymn: "Let Us Break Bread Together")

Words & Chords: Secretary Michael

We can get things to hap-pen, yes___ we can. We can

get things to hap-pen, yes___ we can. When each

wo - man, when each man work to - ge - ther___ hand in hand, we can

get things to hap-pen, yes___ we can.

134. We Mean "Will You Love Me?"

(From the Solo Edition of the Secular Hymnal - key lowered from Eb to D)

Words & Chords: Secretary Michael

Tune: "Gordon" byAdoniram Judson Gordon, 1876
(traditional hymn: "My Jesus I Love Thee I Know Thou Art Mine")

We mean "Will you love me?" what - e - ver we say. We

mean "Will you love me?" and say it all day. To

e - v'ry - one e - v'ry - where in words not al - ways clear. For

"Yes, I will love you" is what we want to hear.

135. We're Not Alone

(From the Solo Edition of the Secular Hymnal - key lowered from D to C)

Words & Chords: Secretary Michael

Tune: "Londonderry Air" (traditional Irish melody)
(traditional hymn: "I Cannot Tell")

We're not a - lone when ants are march-ing in a line. We're not a - lone when blos-soms buzz with bees. We're not a - lone when rab - bits munch on dan - de - lions. We're not a - lone when birds sing in the trees. We're not a - lone when bears are snor - ing in their caves. We're not a - lone when dogs play with their bones. We're not a - lone when whales leap up a - bove the waves. Oh may we ne - ver, ne - ver, ne - ver be a - lone.

136. We're Not At Our Best

(From the Solo Edition of the Secular Hymnal - key unchanged)

Tune: "St. Denio" (Welsh melody)
(traditional hymn: "Immortal, Invisible, God Only Wise")

Words & Chords: Secretary Michael

We're not at our best___ when liv - ing in fear. With -
out e - nough rest,___ our think - ing's not clear. We
must con - front fear, must con - front it to - day. If
we can't have peace,___ then we can - not stay.

137. We're Parents of a Soldier

(From the Solo Edition of the Secular Hymnal - key lowered from Bb to G)

Words & Chords: Secretary Michael

Tune: "Battle Hymn of the Republic" (a camp-meeting tune)
(traditional hymn: "Mine Eyes Have Seen the Glory")

G   **C**

1. We're pa-rents of a sol-dier whe-ther know-ing it or not. And which - e - ver side they're on, they are the
2. We put them in a si - tu - a - tion no - bo - dy could win, as we teach them how to kill and then how
3. If we in-deed were lov-ing par-ents we would be the ones who would take a - way their bul-lets and would

G   **G^maj7/F#**   **Em**   **B**   **Em/D**

sol - dier that we got. If we have the chance to stop them but we ne - ver have them stop, good
kill - ing is a sin. When they come out so con-fused that we're a - fraid to let them in, good
take a - way their guns, 'cuz we don't want pho - ny he - roes, we want daugh-ters, we want sons, so

Am   **D^7**   **G**   **G**   **C**

par - ents we are not. We are par-ents of a sol - dier. We are par-ents of a
par - ents we are not. We are par-ents of a sol - dier. We are par-ents of a
we must be the ones. We are par-ents of a sol - dier. We are par-ents of a

G   **B^+**   **Em**   **Am**   **D^7**   **G**

sol - dier. We are par-ents of a sol - dier. Good par - ents we are not.
sol - dier. We are par-ents of a sol - dier. Good par - ents we are not.
sol - dier. We are par-ents of a sol - dier, so we must be the ones.

138. What Are We Doing?

(From the Solo Edition of the Secular Hymnal - key lowered from D to C)

Words & Chords: Secretary Michael

Tune: "Macchabaeus" by George Frederick Handel, 1747
(traditional hymn: "Thine Be the Glory")

C   Am   Dm   G   C   Am

1. "What are we do - ing here on pla - net earth?" chirps the lit - tle chi - cken,
2. "What are we do - ing here on pla - net earth?" buz - zes the mo - squi - to,

7   Dm   G⁷   C   Am   E   Am   Dm   E

pon - der - ing its birth. Oinks the_ lit - tle pig - let, snorts the car - i - bou,
pon - der - ing its birth. Croaks the_ fa - ther bull - frog, hoots the wise old owl,

13   Am   D⁷   Em   D⁷   G   G⁷

e - ven Mis - ses Cow asks: "Moo, moo,_ moo, moo - moo?"
e - ven_ Cou - sin Cat asks: "Meow, meow, meow, meow meow?"

17   C   Am   Dm   G

"What are we do - ing here_ on_ pla - net earth?"
"What are we do - ing here_ on_ pla - net earth?"

21   C   Am   Dm   G⁷   C

que - stions_ from us crea - tures, pon - der - ing our birth.
que - stions_ from us crea - tures, pon - der - ing our birth.

139. When Feeling Lost

(From the Solo Edition of the Secular Hymnal - key lowered from Em to Dm)

Words & Chords: Secretary Michael

Tune: "Kingsfold" (a traditional English melody)
(traditional hymn: "O Sing a Song of Bethlehem")

| Dm | Bb | Dm | Gm | Dm | Gm | C |

1. When feel - ing lost, when stars are crossed, there's some-thing we__ must do: Jump
2. When feel - ing queer and full of fear, there's some-thing we__ must do: Jump

5 | Dm | Bb | Dm | Gm | Dm | Gm | Dm |

up and down and spin a - round, then__ go learn some - thing new. New__
up and down and spin a - round, then__ go meet some - one new. New__

9 | Am | Dm⁷ | Gm | A | Dm | Gm | C |

skill, new sport,_ new point of view, a - ny - thing will do. Jump_
friend to talk__ and lis - ten to, a - ny - one will do. Jump_

13 | Dm | Bb | Dm | Gm | Dm | Gm | Dm |

up and down_ and__ spin a - round, then__ go learn some - thing new.
up and down_ and__ spin a - round, then__ go meet some - one new.

140. When I Am Down

(From the Solo Edition of the Secular Hymnal - key lowered from A to F)

Words & Chords: Secretary Michael

Tune: Traditional African-American spiritual
(traditional hymn: "Down to the River to Pray")

REFRAIN

F   F(sus4)   F   F(sus4)   B♭   C

When I am down and I need a lit-tle spark, I can usu-al-ly get it at the

8

F   Am   Dm   Dm7   B♭   C7   F

park where I can walk a-round and round un-til ba-lance is found.____

VERSES

17

C   C7   F   Dm   B♭   F

Hey, who is that I see?__ It's my BOSS,__ come to walk with me.__
Hey, who is that I see?__ It's my PAR-ENTS, come to walk with me.__
Hey, who is that I see?__ It's my FRIEND, come to walk with me.__

25

C   C7   F   Dm   B♭   C7   F

Let's walk and talk un-til___ we feel__ peace-ful and still._____
Let's walk and talk un-til___ we feel__ peace-ful and still._____
Let's walk and talk un-til___ we feel__ peac-ful and still._____

141. When Playing Cards

(From the Solo Edition of the Secular Hymnal - key lowered from Bb to A)

Words & Chords: Secretary Michael

Tune: *"O Store Gud"* (a Swedish folk tune)
(traditional hymn: "How Great Thou Art")

When play-ing cards, not e-v'ry hand's a win-ner, not e-v'ry hand is full of kings and queens. When play-ing cards, don't call out "saint" or "sin-ner", be-cause no hand is e-ver what it seems. When play-ing cards, some hands will go a-stray, but that's o-kay, they're dealt that way. When play-ing cards, there's lots of suf-fer-ing, and that is why this song we sing.

142. Who's My Neighbor?

(From the Solo Edition of the Secular Hymnal - key lowered from D to Bb)

Words & Chords: Secretary Michael

Tune: "Victory" by Palestrina, 1588
(traditional hymn: "The Strife Is O'er")

Who's my neigh - bor? Who's my neigh - bor? Who's my neigh - bor?

The an-swer now is ve - ry clear. It's those in need, and those in fear.

Whe-ther they're far, or whe-ther they're near. They're my neigh - bor.

They're my neigh - bor. They're my neigh - bor. They're my neigh - bor.

143. Why Does This Phrase Have Five Measures?

(From the Solo Edition of the Secular Hymnal - key lowered from D to Bb)

Words & Chords: Secretary Michael

Tune: "Lauda Anima" by John Goss, 1869
(traditional hymn: "Praise My Soul the King of Heaven")

Why does this phrase have five mea - sures? All the
o - thers just have four. Why do peo - ple some - times
trea - sure songs that o - thers just ig - nore? Mu - sic
is a deep, deep o - cean, so much deep - er than the score.

144. You Took the One Road

(From the Solo Edition of the Secular Hymnal - key lowered from G to Eb)

Words & Chords: Secretary Michael

Tune: "Loch Lomand"
a traditional Scottish folk song

Oh you took the one road and I took the o - ther, but_____ here at the end we're to - ge - ther. Dif - f'rent lives, dif - f'rent faiths, dif - f'rent coun - tries dif - f'rent wea - ther, but_____ here at the end we're to - ge - ther.

This table is useful for matching traditional hymns to their corresponding Secular Hymns.

TRADITIONAL TO SECULAR
CORRELATION TABLE

Traditional Hymn	*Secular Hymn*
A Mighty Fortress Is Our God	1. A Beauty Hides In Everyone
Aberystwyth	80. People are More
Abide With Me	6. All Need To Feel Significant
Adelaide	75. Pain Can Cause
All Creatures Of Our God and King	101. Them Over There
All Hail the Power of Jesus' Name	17. Communication is the Answer
All in the April Evening	68. Nonviolence Must Be Taught
All My Hope On God is Founded	62. Long Road
All People That On Earth Do Dwell	47. I'm Marching, Marching
All Praise to Him who Reigns Above	107. There's a Better Way
All Things Bright and Beautiful	108. There's a Road Between Our Lands
All to Christ	102. There Are Times
Alleluia! Sing to Jesus	56. Land of Gray
Alleluia, Alleluia Hearts to Heaven	123. Towards a World That Has No Guns
And Can It Be	45. I Will Look and I Will See
And Did Those Feet in Ancient Time	98. The Greatest Walk
Angel Voices Ever Singing	130. We Are People, Plastic People
Angel's Story	5. Achieving Disagreement
Angels From the Realms of Glory	113. Tick-Tock
Arise, My Soul, Arise!	122. Together for So Long
Arizona	35. Harvesting Hunger
Assurance	48. In The End
At the Cross	3. A Peaceful Walk
At the Lamb's High Feast	25. Every Space for Every Face
At the Name of Jesus	15. Climbing Up the Mountain
Azmon	53. I've Never Known a Sinner
Battle Hymn of the Republic	137. We're Parents of a Soldier
Be Still My Soul	99. The Many Truths
Be Thou My Vision	132. We Can Be Tolerant
Beautiful Savior	81. People We Need to Meet
Bethany	85. Seen, Heard and Understood
Billing	87. So Many Ways
Bless Thou The Gifts	116. To Live Our Lives Addiction-Free
Blessed Assurance	48. In The End
Blessed Be the Name	107. There's a Better Way
Blessed Name	107. There's a Better Way
Blest Be the Tie That Binds	89. Someday When Guns Are Gone
Blow Ye Trumpet, Blow	122. Together for So Long
Bread of Heaven	90. Someone Should

Traditional Hymn	Secular Hymn
Breathe On Me	36. I Am a Terrorist
Brethren, We Have Met To Worship	84. Rise and Shine
Bring Them In	103. There is a Game
Christ for the World We Sing	57. Let's Make a Right
Christ is Made the Sure Foundation	86. Skating, Skating
Christ is Made the Sure Foundation	113. Tick-Tock
Christ the Lord is Risen Today	18. Crank and Sprocket
Come Down O Love Divine	119. To Those Who Came Before
Come Let Us All Go Down	140. When I Am Down
Come O Spirit, Dwell Among Us	126. Unconscious Bias
Come Thou Almighty King	57. Let's Make a Right
Come Thou Fount of Every Blessing	19. Disassemble Every Gun
Come Thou Fount of Every Blessing	24. Education is our Destination
Come Thou Long Expected Jesus	56. Land of Gray
Come To The Savior Make No Delay	44. I Think I'm Right
Come We That Love the Lord	70. Oh Child Do Not Despair
Come, Holy Ghost (*Lambillotte*)	30. For What I've Done
Consolation	28. Everything's Changing
Coronation	17. Communication is the Answer
Crown Him With Many Crowns	104. There is a Rule of Thumb
Crucifer	115. To Find a Place
Crusader's Hymn	81. People We Need to Meet
Cwm Rhondda	90. Someone Should
Danny Boy	135. We're Not Alone
Darwall's 148th	121. Today's the Day
Day of Judgment! Day of Wonders!	62. Long Road
Dear Lord and Father of Mankind	52. It's Great To Know Some Things By Heart
Deus Tuorum Militum	116. To Live Our Lives Addiction-Free
Diademata	104. There is a Rule of Thumb
Dix	96. Swapping Shoes
Down Ampney	119. To Those Who Came Before
Down To The River To Pray	140. When I Am Down
Dundee	31. Go Further Farther
Ebenezer	126. Unconscious Bias
Eine Feste Burg	1. A Beauty Hides In Everyone
Endless Song	127. Unless There's No-One Watching
Eternal Father Strong to Save	2. A Long Long Way We've Come Today
Eventide	6. All Need To Feel Significant
Fairest Lord Jesus	81. People We Need to Meet
Faith of Our Fathers	13. Building a Door
Fight the Good Fight	95. Striving To Be
Finlandia (Sibelius)	99. The Many Truths
For All the Saints	112. This Day, This Day
For the Beauty of the Earth	96. Swapping Shoes
Foundation	63. Make Just One Brand New Friend

Traditional Hymn	Secular Hymn
From All That Dwell Below The Skies	101. Them Over There
Garden	58. Let's Ride In Our Time Machines
Glorious Things of Thee are Spoken	73. Open, Open Up the Window
God Be With You Till We Meet Again	54. Journey Forward
God Moves in a Mysterious Way	31. Go Further Farther
Going Home	124. Trusting You, Trusting Me
Guide Me, O Thou Great Jehovah	90. Someone Should
Hail Holy Queen Enthroned Above	21. Don't Choose Sides
Hamburg	92. Standing At Bat
Hanover	110. There's More Than One Way
Hanson Place	46. If We're Not the Ones
Hark! Tis the Shepherd's Voice I Hear	103. There is a Game
Have Thine Own Way, Lord	75. Pain Can Cause
He Who Would Valiant Be	55. Just Because
Helmsley	49. Informed People
Hendon	69. Nothing's Heavy with Lots of Hands
Here is Love, Vast as the Ocean	38. I Declare a Brand-New Me
His Eye is on the Sparrow	60. Let's Stop Making Weapons
Holy God We Praise Thy Name	71. Ojalá
Holy Manna	84. Rise and Shine
Holy, Holy Holy	14. Climbing Up The Ladder
Horsley	117. To Make The World A Better Place
How Can I Keep From Singing?	127. Unless There's No-One Watching
How Firm a Foundation	63. Make Just One Brand New Friend
How Great Thou Art	141. When Playing Cards
How Sweet the Name of Jesus Sounds	40. I Have a Puzzle of the World
Hyfrydol	56. Land of Gray
I Bind Unto Myself Today	118. To Soldiers Lost
I Cannot Tell	135. We're Not Alone
I Come to the Garden Alone	58. Let's Ride In Our Time Machines
I Heard the Voice of Jesus Say	139. When Feeling Lost
I Love Thy Kingdom, Lord	70. Oh Child Do Not Despair
I Need Thee Ev'ry Hour	83. Relieving Suffering
I Surrender All	42. I Surrender
I to the Hills Will Lift My Eyes	31. Go Further Farther
I Vow to Thee My Country	59. Let's Start a Big Commotion
I Will Sing the Wondrous Story	131. We Are Searching
Immaculate Mary	41. I Once Was So Certain
Immortal, Invisible, God Only Wise	136. We're Not At Our Best
In Heavenly Love Abiding	4. Accommodating Others
In the Garden	58. Let's Ride In Our Time Machines
It Is Well With My Soul	22. Don't Know How I Got Here
Italian Hymn	57. Let's Make a Right
Jerusalem	98. The Greatest Walk
Jesus Christ is Risen Today	18. Crank and Sprocket

Traditional Hymn	Secular Hymn
Jesus Lover Of My Soul	80. People are More
Jesus Loves Me This I Know	93. Step by Step
Jesus Paid It All	102. There Are Times
Jesus Shall Reign Where'er The Sun	64. May We Make Moments of Peace
Jesus, Thou Divine Companion	27. Everyone Must Make a Living
Join All the Glorious Names	121. Today's the Day
Joyful, Joyful	123. Towards a World That Has No Guns
Just A Closer Walk With Thee	8. All the Seven Deadly Sins
Kingsfold	139. When Feeling Lost
Largo from Dvorak's "New World Symphony"	124. Trusting You, Trusting Me
Lasst Uns Erfreuen	101. Them Over There
Lauda Anima	143. Why Does This Phrase Have Five Measures?
Lead Us Heavenly Father Lead Us	77. Past Performance is No Guarantee
Lenox	122. Together for So Long
Let All Mortal Flesh Keep Silence	10. Bad is Not a Name
Let Us Break Bread Together	133. We Can Get Things To Happen
Lift High The Cross	115. To Find a Place
Lo He Comes With Clouds Descending	49. Informed People
Lo He Comes With Clouds Descending	113. Tick-Tock
Lobe Den Herren	82. People Will Change
Loch Lomond	144. You Took the One Road
Londonderry Air	135. We're Not Alone
Lord Of All Being	35. Harvesting Hunger
Lord of the Dance	114. 'Tis a Gift
Lord, Enthroned in Heavenly Splendor	94. Storms Will Come
Lourdes Hymn	41. I Once Was So Certain
Love Divine, All Loves Excelling	56. Land of Gray
Love Unknown	20. Diversity in Thought
Lyons	9. Assuming There's Peace
Macchabeus	138. What Are We Doing?
Majestic Sweetness Sits Enthroned	117. To Make The World A Better Place
Make Me a Captive, Lord	104. There is a Rule of Thumb
Marines Hymn	11. Because Violence Can't End Violence
Meine Hoffnung Stehet Feste	62. Long Road
Melita	2. A Long Long Way We've Come Today
Mine Eyes Have Seen The Glory	137. We're Parents of a Soldier
My Hope Is Built On Nothing Less	39. I Have a Garden in the Park
My Jesus I Love Thee I Know Thou Art Mine	134. We Mean "Will You Love Me?"
My Song Is Love Unknown	20. Diversity in Thought
Nearer My God To Thee	85. Seen, Heard and Understood
Need	83. Relieving Suffering
Nettleton	19. Disassemble Every Gun
Nicaea	14. Climbing Up The Ladder
Noël Nouvelet	125. Ultimately We May Not Have Free Will
Now Thank We All Our God	111. Things Are The Way They Are

Traditional Hymn	Secular Hymn
Nun Danket	111. Things Are The Way They Are
O Bless the Lord, My Soul!	70. Oh Child Do Not Despair
O For A Thousand Tongues	53. I've Never Known a Sinner
O God Of Bethel By Whose Hand	31. Go Further Farther
O God of Loveliness	129. Walking in Someone's Shoes
O Jesus I Have Promised	5. Achieving Disagreement
O Love That Wilt Not Let Me Go	51. Intelligence is a Bouquet
O Love, How Deep	116. To Live Our Lives Addiction-Free
O Perfect Love	65. No Cheers For David
O Sacred Head, Sore Wounded	74. Our Garden Full of Flowers
O Sing a Song of Bethlehem	139. When Feeling Lost
O Store Gud	141. When Playing Cards
O the Deep Deep Love of Jesus	126. Unconscious Bias
Ode to Joy (Beethoven)	123. Towards a World That Has No Guns
Oh Worship The King	9. Assuming There's Peace
Old Hundredth	47. I'm Marching, Marching
Once to Every Man and Nation	126. Unconscious Bias
Onward Christian Soldiers	72. Onward, Upward
Our God Our Help In Ages Past	100. The Only Path to Peace is Peace
Our Great Savior	56. Land of Gray
Peace Like a River	79. Peace Like a River
Penlan	4. Accommodating Others
Picardy	10. Bad is Not a Name
Pleading Savior	27. Everyone Must Make a Living
Poor Wayfaring Man of Grief	37. I Am the Captain of My Boat
Praise God from Whom all Blessings Flow	47. I'm Marching, Marching
Praise My Soul The King Of Heaven	143. Why Does This Phrase Have Five Measures?
Praise the Lord, Ye Heavens	56. Land of Gray
Praise to God, Immortal Praise	96. Swapping Shoes
Praise to the Holiest in the Height	87. So Many Ways
Praise To The Lord	82. People Will Change
Redeemed	67. Nonviolence May Take a Long Time
Regent Square	113. Tick-Tock
Rejoice, The Lord Is King	121. Today's the Day
Repton	52. It's Great To Know Some Things By Heart
Revive Us Again	109. There's Claim Number One
Rhosymedre	20. Diversity in Thought
Ring Out The Old, Ring In The New	116. To Live Our Lives Addiction-Free
Rise Up, O Men of God!	70. Oh Child Do Not Despair
Rock Of Ages	33. Grief Has Got To Take Its Time
Royal Oak	108. There's a Road Between Our Lands
Salve Regina	21. Don't Choose Sides
Salzburg	25. Every Space for Every Face
Shall We Gather At The River	46. If We're Not the Ones
Simple Gifts	114. 'Tis a Gift

Traditional Hymn	Secular Hymn
Since Jesus Came Into My Heart	32. Going Up, Going Up
Sine Nomine	112. This Day, This Day
Sing of Mary	27. Everyone Must Make a Living
Singing Songs of Expectation	126. Unconscious Bias
Slane	132. We Can Be Tolerant
Soldiers of Christ, Arise	104. There is a Rule of Thumb
Sparrow	60. Let's Stop Making Weapons
St. Gertrude	72. Onward, Upward
St. Helen	94. Storms Will Come
St. Patrick's Breastplate	118. To Soldiers Lost
St. Thomas	70. Oh Child Do Not Despair
Still, Still With Thee	28. Everything's Changing
Surrender	42. I Surrender
Sutra Hymn	23. Each Little Raindrop
Take My Life and Let It Be	69. Nothing's Heavy with Lots of Hands
Tell Me The Old Old Story	61. Let's Try Something Different
The Church's One Foundation	105. There is an Empty Box
The Day Thou Gavest Lord Is Ended	50. Injustice to You is Injustice to Me
The Jubilee	122. Together for So Long
The King Of Love My Shepherd Is	97. Tall Oaks From Little Acorns Grow
The Lord Is King, Lift Up Thy Voice	116. To Live Our Lives Addiction-Free
The Old Rugged Cross	106. There is Something Wrong
The Solid Rock	2. A Long Long Way We've Come Today
The Solid Rock	39. I Have a Garden in the Park
The Strife is O'er	142. Who's My Neighbor?
There is a Balm in Gilead	26. Everybody Has Their Issues
There Is A Green Hill Far Away	117. To Make The World A Better Place
Thine Be The Glory (Handel)	138. What Are We Doing?
Thy Strong Word Did Cleave the Darkness	126. Unconscious Bias
Tis a Gift	114. 'Tis a Gift
Tis So Sweet to Trust in Jesus	34. Happy Be
To God Be The Glory	7. All Praise to the Troubled
Ton-y-Botel	126. Unconscious Bias
Toplady	33. Grief Has Got To Take Its Time
Trentham	36. I Am a Terrorist
Trust And Obey	120. Today Is My Day
Trust in Jesus	34. Happy Be
Turn Your Eyes Upon Jesus	43. I Think I Could Work in a Castle
Twimfina	12. Borders, Boundaries, Walls and Fences
Twimfina	16. Come Live With Us
Victory	142. Who's My Neighbor?
Ville Du Havre	22. Don't Know How I Got Here
Wachet Auf	128. Wake, Awake
Wake, Awake, for Night is Flying	128. Wake, Awake
Warrenton	24. Education is our Destination

Traditional Hymn	Secular Hymn
We Cannot Measure How You Heal	29. For Those Who Have Beliefs Bizarre
We Have and Anchor	88. Some Are Young, Some Old
We Plough The Fields And Scatter	66. No Need To Sing The Same Notes
We Rest on Thee	99. The Many Truths
Were You There?	91. Spent Our Treasure
Westminster Abbey	86. Skating, Skating
What a Friend We Have in Jesus	78. Peace Is Not What I Looked For
What Thanks and Praise To Thee We Owe	116. To Live Our Lives Addiction-Free
What Wondrous Love is This	76. Parents Gone
When I Survey the Wondrous Cross	92. Standing At Bat
When Peace Like a River	22. Don't Know How I Got Here
Will Your Anchor Hold	88. Some Are Young, Some Old
Wondrous Love	76. Parents Gone
Wye Valley	15. Climbing Up The Mountain
Ye Banks and Braes	29. For Those Who Have Beliefs Bizarre
Ye Servants of God	110. There's More Than One Way

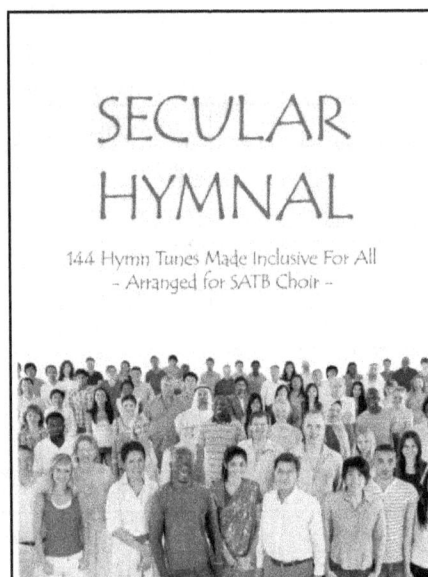

The *SATB Edition* of the Secular Hymnal (shown above) is a complete compilation of all 12 of the "Roadway" booklets shown on the facing page. The SATB Edition is best for choirs, quartets, friends and families who like to sing in harmony. It's also great for students of music theory and counterpoint.

Your *Solo Edition* of the Secular Hymnal is best for individual singers and groups that sing in unison. It contains the soprano (melody) lines and nice large chord symbols to all 144 Secular Hymns. Since there's no more worry about squashing the alto, tenor and bass voices, the Solo Edition contains melody lines that are in a lower, more comfortable range for us everyday singers.

159

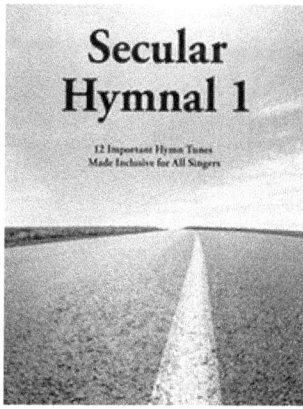

Secular Hymnal 1

12 Important Hymn Tunes
Made Inclusive for All Singers

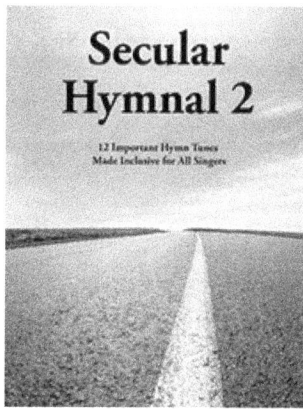

Secular Hymnal 2

12 Important Hymn Tunes
Made Inclusive for All Singers

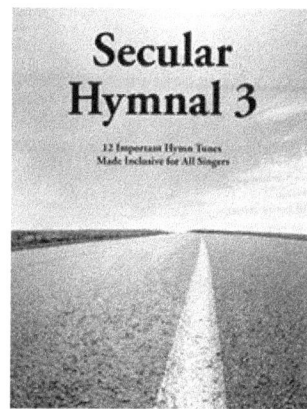

Secular Hymnal 3

12 Important Hymn Tunes
Made Inclusive for All Singers

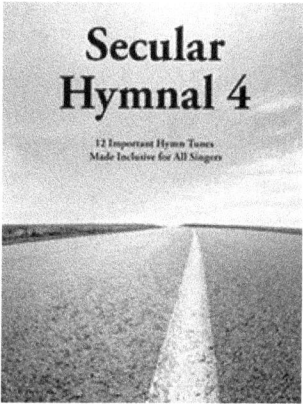

Secular Hymnal 4

12 Important Hymn Tunes
Made Inclusive for All Singers

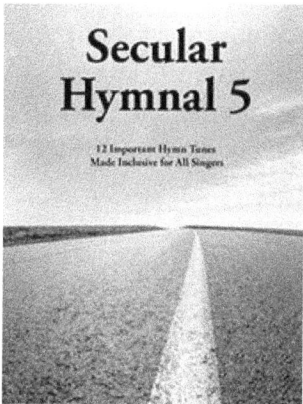

Secular Hymnal 5

12 Important Hymn Tunes
Made Inclusive for All Singers

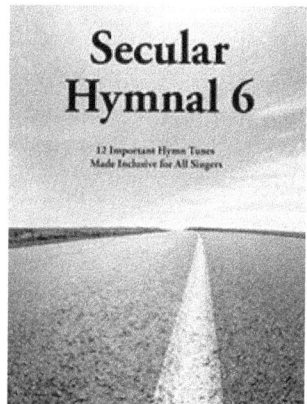

Secular Hymnal 6

12 Important Hymn Tunes
Made Inclusive for All Singers

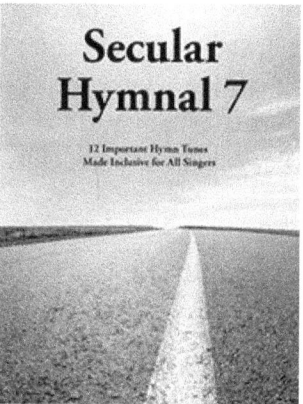

Secular Hymnal 7

12 Important Hymn Tunes
Made Inclusive for All Singers

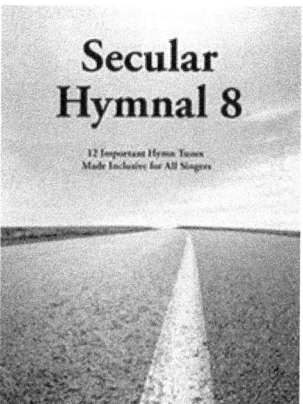

Secular Hymnal 8

12 Important Hymn Tunes
Made Inclusive for All Singers

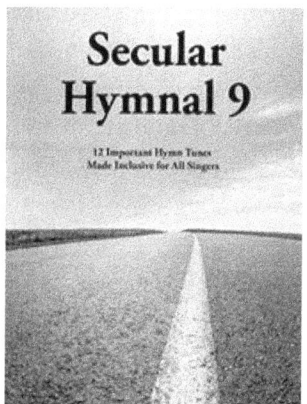

Secular Hymnal 9

12 Important Hymn Tunes
Made Inclusive for All Singers

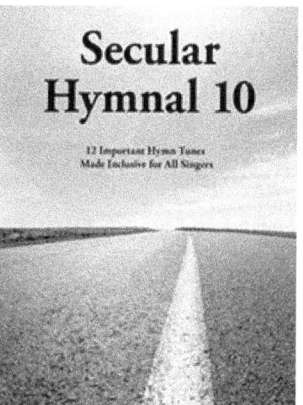

Secular Hymnal 10

12 Important Hymn Tunes
Made Inclusive for All Singers

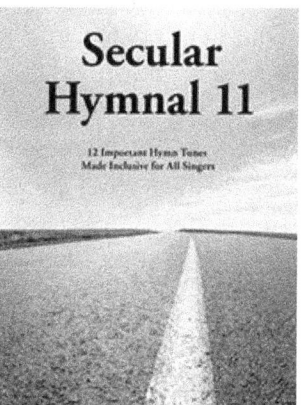

Secular Hymnal 11

12 Important Hymn Tunes
Made Inclusive for All Singers

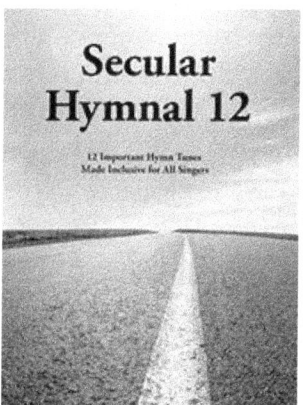

Secular Hymnal 12

12 Important Hymn Tunes
Made Inclusive for All Singers

PERSONAL NOTES AND EXPLANATIONS

LYRICS

When I was a public school music teacher, I was made *very* aware that church hymns were inappropriate for the classroom. I was careful to never cross that line. At the same time, I knew from personal experience how useful hymn singing is for building musicianship, for tightening-up a choir, and for learning to sight-read. There is something special about hymns - they're like musical vitamins. This is the reason why I wrote the Secular Hymnal. By substituting all religious content with lyrics that everybody would feel comfortable with, we classroom teachers could have our cake and eat it too. We could make use of our heritage of chorale music without violating the religious sensitivities of others.

Lyrics are always "about" something. What should I write about that would be appropriate to this revered music? I certainly couldn't write 144 sets of lyrics about "oatmeal". And I have zero appetite for sugary, meaningless lyrics with contrived rhymes. As I hope you will discover, all the lyrics in this book are *about* something, with "Peace" and "Equality" being among the predominant themes. I hope that you find these new verses to be worthy substitutes for the much loved verses that they replace.

WORD DIVISION

As for dividing words into syllables, I used to be a purest about dividing words so that each syllable began with a consonant. It made sense because that's how the tongue, teeth and lips work in the mouth to actually form the syllables. And so I was strict about it and paid no regard to how words are conventionally divided in the dictionary. But even though my syllabification may have been "anatomically" correct, I began to realize that it might not always result in good communication. Maybe singers won't be able to immediately grasp the meaning of a word when it is divided unconventionally. So now I'm no longer a purist - not even always consistent. I still prefer to begin syllables with a consonant, but I'll happily start with a vowel if it might make communication more clear. For example, words ending with the suffix "-ing" will probably be written that way (without a consonant) simply because they seem easier to read.

CHANGES TO THE TRADITIONAL MUSIC

I feel an obligation to not change a hymn's melody line. And so the hymn tunes in the Secular Hymnals usually sound exactly the same as the hymn tunes in any other hymnal. The whole purpose of the Secular Hymnal project is to shape new lyrics to the original tunes, not the other way around. Occasionally I may need to make insignificant changes (for example, changing a quarter note to two eighths to accommodate an extra syllable - or vice versa). On rare occasions I might repeat a section. But these minor changes seldom effect the integrity of the original hymn tune.

I don't feel much allegiance to the "original" key. Being a choir singer myself, I always try to make the singers as comfortable as possible. Who in the world wants to sing outside his or her range? As I see it, my duty is to find the most comfortable key regardless of how it was originally written.

In this book (the *Solo Edition* of the Secular Hymnal), the absence of the bass, tenor and alto voices means that the melody no longer has to be forced up so high. And so I've lowered the key for almost all of the hymns. If you feel that I overdid it and lowered any of them too much, just raise them back up. (In fact in this revised edition, I've raised several myself.) All in all, I hope that you find the key changes to be more comfortable.

SOURCES

Although I researched all of the hymns, none of the research was "primary" research. Instead I've relied entirely on established sources for my information. The internet is rich with hymn source material and information (such as "www.hymnary.org") for which I am very grateful. For note-by-note transcription of the old hymns into secular hymns, I more often than not relied on my own copy of "The Christian Life Hymnal" [2012 Printing]. I appreciate its crisp scores and its clear references.

Choice of Hymns: In choosing which traditional hymns to transform into secular hymns, my objective was to find tunes that people considered "favorites". It's largely from the many published lists of "favorite hymns" that the tunes for the Secular Hymnal were chosen. They were chosen for their diversity, importance, and above all beauty.

Errors: Having checked and double-checked countless times, I'm tempted to claim that there aren't any mistakes left anywhere in the book. But I know better than to say something so stupid. So if you find any errors, please let me know so that I may correct them.

COPYRIGHT

To my knowledge I have violated no copyright claims. If you find that I have inadvertently violated someone's copyright, please let me know and I will make the necessary changes immediately. (Personally I find that our current copyright laws last way too long and are unreasonably restrictive. I suggest that composers choose a "Creative Commons" category or just put their material into the public domain as I do).

TYPESETTING

The Secular Hymnal's **notation** was created using Sibelius 6 (font: Keyboard Helsinki with Georgia text). The Secular Hymnal's **text** was created using Adobe InDesign CS6 (font: Adobe Garamond Pro).

SOLO EDITION RECORDINGS

Piano renditions of all secular hymn tunes and chords have been recorded and are available free online (www.secularhymnal.com). Singers are welcome to post their own YouTube recordings.

SOLO EDITION CHORDS

I tried to pick chords that were clean, necessary and functional. I hope that you like them, but of course you are welcome to select different harmonies. I also hope that you like the large chord symbols (14 pt. bold).

NOTES ON THE INDIVIDUAL HYMNS

These notes are taken from the <u>SATB Edition</u> of the Secular Hymnal. Since you are using the <u>Solo Edition</u> (melody and chords only), you will find some of the information (regarding the choral arrangements) to be irrelevant.

1. <u>A Beauty Hides in Everyone</u>:
This Secular Hymn is built on the 1529 song "Ein Feste Burg" written by none other than Martin Luther himself. Nowadays the tune is best known as the hymn "A Mighty Fortress Is Our God" [#22 in the Christian Life Hymnal], which is the source that I used.
Topic of Song: finding beauty in everyone;

2. <u>A Long Long Way We've Come Today</u>:
This Secular Hymn is built on the tune "Melita" by John Bacchus Dykes in 1861. Today the tune is best known by the hymns "The Solid Rock" [#411 in the Christian Life Hymnal], and "Eternal Father, Strong to Save" [#600 in the Christian Life Hymnal] which is the source that I used.
Topic of Song: creating peace is an accomplishment worth celebrating;

3. <u>A Peaceful Walk</u>:
This Secular Hymn is based on a tune composed by Ralph E Hudson. Later the hymn "At the Cross" [#525 in the Christian Life Hymnal] was created from the tune, which is the source that I used.
Topic of Song: peace / nonviolence;

4. <u>Accommodating Others</u>:
This Secular Hymn is based on the tune "Penlan" written by David Jenkins in 1898. It is more commonly known today as the hymn "In Heavenly Love Abiding" [found on the website "hymnary.org], which is the source that I used.
Topic of Song: strong people are those who accommodate others;

5. <u>Achieving Disagreement</u>:
This Secular Hymn is built on the tune "Angel's Story", written by Arthur Henry Mann in 1881. Today it is more commonly known as the hymn "O Jesus I Have Promised" [#446 in the Christian Life Hymnal], which is the source that I used.
Topic of Song: respectful disagreement can be something positive;

6. <u>All Need To Feel Significant</u>:
This Secular Hymn is based on the 1861 tune "Eventide" composed by William Henry Monk, which was subsequently used for the hymn "Abide With Me" [#575 in the Christian Life Hymnal] which is the source that I used.
Topic of Song: seeing others as ourselves;

7. <u>All Praise to the Troubled</u>:
This Secular Hymn is based on the 1875 Hymn "To God Be the Glory [#31 in the Christian Life Hymnal] written by William Howard Doane, which is the source that I used.
Topic of Song: accepting others, seeing personality differences as a positive;

8. <u>All the Seven Deadly Sins</u>:
This Secular Hymn is based on a traditional folksong which is now popularly known as the hymn "Just a Closer Walk With Thee" [#461 in the Christian Life Hymnal] which is the source that I used.
Topic of Song: humorous hymn about "wrath, gluttony, envy, pride, greed, sloth, and lust";

9. <u>Assuming There's Peace</u>:
This Secular Hymn is built on the tune "Lyons", written by Johann Michael Haydn (the younger brother of Joseph Haydn) in 1770. It was later arranged by William Gardiner in 1815. It is popularly known today as the hymn "O Worship the King" [#10 in the Christian Life Hymnal], which is the source that I used.
Topic of Song: acting as if there were peace is a good strategy for creating peace;

10. <u>"Bad" is Not a Name</u>:
This Secular Hymn is built on a traditional French tune titled "Picardy". It is popular today as the hymn "Let All Mortal Flesh Keep Silence". It can be found as Hymn #82 in the Christian Life Hymnal and as Hymn #46 in the Book of Catholic Worship (1966 Edition). However in these and in other hymnals, the song curiously only occurs as a unison melody. So to be consistent with the other hymns, I decided to harmonize it and arrange it as a 4-part chorale.
Topic of Song: avoid labeling people;

11. <u>Because Violence Can't End Violence</u>:
This Secular Hymn is built on a melody that seems to have started in the 1867 Jacques Offenbach opera buffa titled: "Geneviève de Brabant" (Genevieve of Brabant). The song (Gendarmes' Duet) was a duet between two police officers. But it is much more popularly known today as the Marines' Hymn ("From the Halls of Montezuma"). I arranged it as an SATB chorale.
Topic of Song: there are better ways to resolve disputes;

12. <u>Borders, Boundaries, Walls and Fences</u>:
This Secular Hymn is taken from my musical "Twimfina". It's not structured like a hymn, but I included it simply because I like it so much. In fact the refrain "The World Is My Family, I'm Not Afraid" makes the acronym "TWIMFINA", the name of the play.
Topic of Song: the world is my family, I'm not afraid;

13. <u>Building a Door</u>:
This Secular Hymn is built on the tune "St. Catherine" written by Henri F. Henry in 1864 (and arranged by James George Walton in the same year). It is popularly known today as the hymn "Faith Of Our Fathers" [#322 in the Christian Life Hymnal], which is the source that I used.
Topic of Song: mixing with others is healthful;

14. <u>Climbing Up The Ladder</u>:
This Secular Hymn is based on the tune "Nicaea" written by John Bacchus Dykes in 1861. It is known everywhere as the famous hymn "Holy, Holy, Holy" [#1 in the Christian Life Hymnal], which is the source that I used.
Topic of Song: seeing others as ourselves;

15. <u>Climbing Up The Mountain</u>:
This Secular Hymn is built on the song "Wye Valley", written by James Mountain in 1876. It is popularly known today as the hymn "At the Name of Jesus" [#207 in the Christian Life Hymnal], which is the source that I used.
Topic of Song: no pain, no gain;

16. <u>Come Live With Us</u>:
This Secular Hymn is the Afterword in my musical "Twimfina".
Topic of Song: living in a "Love Thy Neighbor" world;

17. <u>Communication is the Answer</u>:
This Secular Hymn is based on the tune "Coronation", written by Oliver Holden in 1793. Among the hymns that were subsequently built on the "Coronation" tune is the hymn "All Hail the Power of Jesus' Name" [#57 in the Christian Life Hymnal], which is the source that I used.
Topic of Song: communication;

18. <u>Crank and Sprocket</u>:
This Secular Hymn is based on the tune "Easter Hymn" which can be found in the Lyra Davidson collection of 1708. It is popularly known today as the hymn "Jesus Christ is Risen Today" [#45 in the Book of Catholic Worship - 1966 Edition], which is the source that I used.
Topic of Song: people act the way they are "built", and so we must be kind to everybody;

19. <u>Disassemble Every Gun</u>:
This Secular Hymn is built on the 1813 tune "Nettleton". It is better known today as the hymn "Come Thou Fount of Every Blessing" [#13 in the Christian Life Hymnal] which is the source that I used.
Topic of Song: take apart a gun with a screwdriver and then scatter the parts;

20. <u>Diversity in Thought</u>:
This Secular Hymn is built on the tune "Rhosymedre", written by John Edwards in 1840. It is more commonly known today as the hymn "My Song Is Love Unknown" [#164 in the Christian Life Hymnal], which is the source that I used.
Topic of Song: it's healthful to shake-up our fixed ways from time to time;

21. <u>Don't Choose Sides</u>:
This Secular Hymn is built on the old song "Salve Regina" written in Latin a millennium ago (c.1050). A very popular English setting of the tune is the hymn "Hail Holy Queen Enthroned Above" [#35 in the Book of Catholic Worship - 1966 Edition], which is the source that I used.
Topic of Song: peace / conflict resolution;

22. <u>Don't Know How I Got Here</u>:
This Secular Hymn is built on the 1876 tune "Ville Du Havre" by Philip Paul Bliss. Nowadays the tune is best known as the hymn "It Is Well With My Soul" also known by the beginning words "When Peace Like a River" [#363 in the Christian Life Hymnal], which is the source that I used.
Topic of Song: accepting life;

23. <u>Each Little Raindrop</u>:
This Secular Hymn isn't based on a traditional hymn. Hoping to have a diversity of hymns in my collection, I composed this with a "Buddhist" flavor and titled it "Sutra Hymn". The pentatonic scale gives it that Asian sound. Later when I was writing new lyrics to all the hymns, this hymn was among them.
Topic of Song: "What if everybody did that?" (Immanuel Kant's "Categorial Imperative")

24. Education Is Our Destination:
This Secular Hymn is based on the old song "Warrenton", which is found in the 1844 Sacred Harp book. Among the modern hymns built on the "Warrenton" tune is "Come Thou Fount of Every Blessing" [#14 in the Christian Life Hymnal]. I could find no arrangements free of copyright protection, so I arranged it myself to sound like a train.
Topic of Song: right to an education;

25. Every Space for Every Face:
This Secular Hymn is built on the tune "Salzburg", written by Jacob Hintze in 1678. It was later harmonized by none other than J.S. Bach. Today it is popularly known as the hymn "At the Lamb's High Feast We Sing [#326 in the Christian Life Hymnal], which is the source that I used.
Topic of Song: certain parts of life should not be sectored off for certain "types" of people;

26. Everybody Has Their Issues:
This Secular Hymn is based on the popular African-American spiritual "There is a Balm in Gilead". I was unable to find any copyright-free arrangements, so I made the SATB arrangement myself and put it in the public domain.
Topic of Song: although some people are good at hiding it, everybody goes through periods of mental instability;

27. Everyone Must Make a Living:
This Secular Hymn is based on the tune "Pleading Savior" by Joshua Leavitt (c.1830). It can also be found as the hymn "Jesus, Thou Divine Companion" [#148 in the Christian Life Hymnal]. However our source is the hymn "Sing of Mary" [#76 in the Book of Catholic Worship - 1966 Edition].
Topic of Song: seeing others as ourselves;

28. Everything's Changing:
This Secular Hymn is built on the 1834 piano composition "Consolation" by Felix Mendelssohn. Today it is popularly known as the hymn "Still, Still With Thee" [#574 in the Christian Life Hymnal] which is the source that I used.
Topic of Song: everything is changing; we can be a part of the change;

29. For Those Who Have Beliefs Bizarre:
This Secular Hymn is based on the traditional Scottish folk tune "Ye Banks and Braes". It is more commonly known as the hymn "We Cannot Measure How You Heal" [which can be found at hymnary.org]. The arrangements are still under copyright protection so I made the SATB arrangement myself and placed it in the public domain.
Topic of Song: accepting people regardless of their strange ideas;

30. For What I've Done:
This Secular Hymn is based on the 1840 hymn "Come Holy Ghost" by Louis Lambillotte. It can be found as Hymn #14 in the Book of Catholic Worship [1966 Edition], which is the source that I used.
Topic of Song: asking for forgiveness;

31. Go Further Farther:
This Secular Hymn is based on a tune from the 1615 Scottish Psalter titled "Dundee". It was harmonized by Thomas Ravenscroft (who lived from 1592 to 1635). It is more commonly known as the hymns: "O God of Bethel By Whose Hand", and "I To the Hills Will Lift My Eyes", and "God Moves in a Mysterious Way". My source for the Dundee arrangement was the online website "hymnary.org".
Topic of Song: keep progressing further and farther;

32. <u>Going Up, Going Up</u>:
This Secular Hymn is built on the tune "McDaniel", written by Charles Hutchinson Gabriel in 1914. Today it is more commonly known as the hymn "Since Jesus Came Into My Heart" [#514 in the Christian Life Hymnal], which is the source that I used.
Topic of Song: motivational;

33. <u>Grief Has Got To Take Its Time</u>:
This Secular Hymn is built on the tune "Toplady" written by Thomas Hastings in 1830. Today it is popularly known as the hymn "Rock of Ages" [#284 in the Christian Life Hymnal], which is the source that I used.
Topic of Song: grief is slow but plays a role;

34. <u>Happy Be</u>:
This Secular Hymn is based on an 1882 song by William James Kirkpatrick titled "Trust in Jesus". It is more popularly known today as the hymn "Tis So Sweet to Trust in Jesus" [#414 in the Christian Life Hymnal], which is the source that I used.
Topic of Song: 12 contemporary beatitudes;

35. <u>Harvesting Hunger</u>:
This Secular Hymn is based on the tune "Arizona", written by Robert Henry Earnshaw (who lived from 1856-1929). Today the tune is more commonly known by the hymn "Lord of All Being" [found online at "hymnary. org"] which is the source that I used.
Topic of Song: the importance of education;

36. <u>I am a Terrorist</u>:
This Secular Hymn is built on the 1888 tune "Trentham" by Robert Jackson. Today the tune is more commonly known by the hymn "Breathe On Me" [#225 in the Christian Life Hymnal], which is the source that I used.
Topic of Song: capital punishment / human condition;

37. <u>I am the Captain of My Boat</u>:
This Secular Hymn is built on the song "A Poor Wayfaring Man of Grief" written by George Coles back around 1880. The Latter Day Saints have a version of it [#29 in their 1985 English Language Hymnal]. I like the jaunty melody, but since the copyright status of the LDS arrangement was not clear, I had to do my own SATB arrangement.
Topic of Song: acceptance of life / anti-pride;

38. <u>I Declare a Brand-New Me</u>:
This Secular Hymn is built on the tune "Cymraeg", written by Robert Lowry in 1876. It is more commonly known today as the hymn "Here is Love Vast as the Ocean" [#254 in the Christian Life Hymnal], which is the source that I used.
Topic of Song: it is healthy to give ourselves a second chance;

39. <u>I Have a Garden in the Park</u>:
This Secular Hymn is built on the tune "Solid Rock" by William Batchelder Bradbury, written in 1863. It is more commonly known today as the hymn "My Hope Is Built On Nothing Less" [#410 in the Christian Life Hymnal], which is the source that I used.
Topic of Song: parks are important, even for homeless people;

40. I Have a Puzzle of the World:
This Secular Hymn is built on the tune "St. Peter" written by Alexander Robert Reinagle in 1836. It is more popularly known today as the hymn "How Sweet the Name of Jesus Sounds" [#399 in the Christian Life Hymnal], which is the source that I used.
Topic of Song: solving the world's problems requires cooperation;

41. I Once Was So Certain:
This Secular Hymn is based on a traditional French tune known as the "Lourdes Hymn". However my source is the hymn "Immaculate Mary" [#43 in the Book of Catholic Worship - 1966 Edition].
Topic of Song: importance of being open and accepting mistakes;

42. I Surrender:
This Secular Hymn is built on the 1896 tune "Surrender" by Winfield Scott Weeden. Nowadays the tune is best known as the hymn "I Surrender All" [#305 in the Christian Life Hymnal], which is the source that I used.
Topic of Song: rejecting shiny things;

43. I Think I Could Work in a Castle:
This Secular Hymn is built on a 1922 tune by Helen Howarth Lemmel. It is more popularly known today as the hymn "Turn Your Eyes Upon Jesus" [#297 in the Christian Life Hymnal], which is the source that I used.
Topic of Song: contentment;

44. I Think I'm Right:
This Secular Hymn is based on a tune written by George Frederick Root in 1870. Today it is known by the hymn "Come to the Savior, Make No Delay" [found at the "cyberhymnal.org" website], which is the source that I used.
Topic of Song: it is very important that we be open to the possibility of being wrong;

45. I Will Look and I Will See:
This Secular Hymn is based on the tune "Sagina", written by Thomas Campbell in 1825. It is popularly known today as the hymn "And Can It Be?" [#247 in the Christian Life Hymnal], which is the source that I used.
Topic of Song: "looking for beauty" is a prerequisite for "finding beauty";

46. If We're Not the Ones:
This Secular Hymn is built on the tune "Hanson Place" written by Robert Lowry in 1864. It is popularly known today as the hymn "Shall We Gather at the River" [#559 in the Christian Life Hymnal], which is the source that I used.
Topic of Song: if we don't do it, it won't get done;

47. I'm Marching, Marching:
This secular hymn is built on the ancient song "Old Hundredth", which is popular today as the hymn "Praise God from Whom all Blessings Flow". More than one version is found in the Christian Life Hymnal. I mixed and matched, using the harmony and arrangement from Hymn #21 but the meter and rhythm from Hymn 621 (to avoid the imprecision of fermatas).
Topic of Song: stepping out of your group;

48. In The End:
This Secular Hymn is built on the 1873 tune "Assurance" by Phoebe Palmer Knapp. Nowadays the tune is best known as the hymn "Blessed Assurance" [#362 in the Christian Life Hymnal], which is the source that I used.
Topic of Song: accepting life, being realistic;

NOTES ON THE INDIVIDUAL HYMNS (continued)

49. Informed People:
This Secular Hymn is built on the traditional English melody "Helmsley". Today the tune is more commonly known as the hymn "Lo He Comes With Clouds Descending" [#211 in the Christian Life Hymnal], which is the source that I used.
Topic of Song: informed people tend to behave more responsibly;

50. Injustice to You is Injustice to Me:
This Secular Hymn is based on the song "St. Clement", written by Clement Cotterill Scholefield in 1874. It is popular today as the hymn "The Day Thou Gavest Lord Is Ended" [#578 in the Christian Life Hymnal], which is the source that I used.
Topic of Song: injustice to one is injustice to all;

51. Intelligence is a Bouquet:
This Secular Hymn is built on the tune "St. Margaret", written by Albert Lister Peace. It is more commonly known today as the hymn "O Love That Will Not Let Me Go" [#389 in the Christian Life Hymnal], which is the source that I used.
Topic of Song: there are many kinds of intelligence;

52. It's Great To Know Some Things By Heart:
This Secular Hymn is built on the tune "Repton" by Charles Hubert Hastings Parry in 1888. It is popularly known today as the unison hymn "Dear Lord and Father of Mankind" [#475 in the Christian Life Hymnal]. Since the Secular Hymns are all in chorale style, I used the melody to create an SATB arrangement.
Topic of Song: the joy of memorizing;

53. I've Never Known a Sinner:
This Secular Hymn is built on the 1828 tune "Azmon" by Carl Gotthelf Glaser. It was arranged in 1839 by Lowell Mason. Nowadays the tune is best known as the hymn "O for a Thousand Tongues to Sing" [#49 in the Christian Life Hymnal], which is the source that I used.
Topic of Song: accepting others, compassion;

54. Journey Forward:
This Secular Hymn is based on the 1880 hymn "God Be With You Till We Meet Again" written by William Tomer [#586 in the Christian Life Hymnal], which is the source that I used.
Topic of Song: importance of education;

55. Just Because:
This Secular Hymn is based on a traditional English tune "Monks Gate". In 1904 Ralph Vaughan Williams arranged it. It is popularly known today as the hymn "He Who Would Valiant Be" (which I was able to find at "openhymnal.org"). The hymn appeared in the movie "Chariots of Fire" and was sung at Margaret Thatcher's funeral. The hymn is very irregular and difficult to learn (and difficult to write new lyrics for). And so I (rightly or wrongly) made some simplifying changes so that it could be squeezed into a regular 4/4 meter, 16-bar chorale format. Sorry Ralph.
Topic of Song: things aren't always they way they're presented - critical thinking is necessary;

56. Land of Gray:
This Secular Hymn is built on the old tune "Hyfrydol" written by Rowland Hugh Prichard around 1830. It is a popular tune for hymns, in fact in the Christian Life Hymnal alone there are 5 hymns that use Hyfrydol as their tune, including "Love Divine, All Loves Excelling" [#42 in the Christian Life Hymnal], which is the source that I used.
Topic of Song: living with diversity;

57. Let's Make a Right:
This Secular Hymn is based on "Italian Hymn", written by Felice de Giardini in 1769. It is popular today as the hymn "Come Thou Almighty King" [#4 in the Christian Life Hymnal], which is the source that I used. The list of "world needs" itemized in this Secular Hymn was gleaned from the film "One Peace at a Time".
Topic of Song: a life of service to others;

58. Let's Ride in our Time Machines:
This Secular Hymn is based on the 1912 tune "Garden" composed by Charles Austin Miles, which became the hymn "In the Garden" [#456 in the Christian Life Hymnal] which is the source that I used.
Topic of Song: accepting life, accepting others, positive attitude;

59. Let's Start a Big Commotion:
This Secular Hymn is built on the music "Thaxted", written by Gustaf Holst in 1921. It is popularly known today as the stirring hymn "I Vow to Thee, My Country" [found at the website "newchurchmusic.org"], which is the source that I used.
Topic of Song: sometimes attention to injustice can only be achieved by making lots of noise;

60. Let's Stop Making Weapons:
This Secular Hymn is built on the 1905 song "Sparrow" by Charles Hutchinson Gabriel. It is popularly known today as the hymn "His Eye is on the Sparrow" [#378 in the Christian Life Hymnal] which is the source that I used.
Topic of Song: against the manufacture of weapons;

61. Let's Try Something Different:
This Secular Hymn is built on the tune "Evangel" written by William Howard Doane in 1867. It is popularly known today as the hymn "Tell Me the Old, Old Story" [#532 in the Christian Life Hymnal], which is the source that I used.
Topic of Song: it is a good lifestyle to constantly learn new things;

62. Long Road:
This Secular Hymn is built on a tune written by Joachim Neander in 1680 (the year the young man died). The tune began with the lyrics: "Meine Hoffnung Stehet Feste" (My Hope Stands Firm). In 1723 it was adapted and harmonized by J.S. Bach for his Cantata 40. Other hymns that use this tune include: "All My Hope On God is Founded" and "Day of Judgment! Day of Wonders!" My source was the website "hymnary.org".
I admit to changing one melody note (the last note of measure 4 and its chord) to give the cadence a more interrogative character.
Topic of Song: perseverance; committing to the long haul;

63. Make Just One Brand-New Friend:
This Secular Hymn is based on the 1832 song "Foundation" by Joseph Funk. It is more commonly known today as the hymn "How Firm a Foundation" [#392 in the Christian Life Hymnal] which is the source that I used.
Topic of Song: the importance of having a diversity of friends;

64. <u>May We Make Moments of Peace</u>:
This Secular Hymn is built on the tune "Duke Street", written by John Hatton in 1793. It is more commonly known today as the hymn "Jesus Shall Reign, Where'er the Sun" [#39 in the Christian Life Hymnal], which is the source that I used.
Topic of Song: little moments accumulate, so create them wisely;

65. <u>No Cheers For David</u>:
This Secular Hymn is built on a the popular hymn "O Perfect Love", written by Joseph Barnby in 1889. It was later arranged by John Stainer in 1898. It can be found as Hymn #546 in the Christian Life Hymnal (which is the source that I used).
Topic of Song: supporting peace is better than supporting war;

66. <u>No Need To Sing The Same Notes</u>:
This Secular Hymn is built on the German song "Wir Pflugen" (We Plow), written by Johann A.P. Schutz in 1800. The English hymn is titled "We Plow The Fields And Scatter", which is the source that I used, having found it at the website "hymnary.org". I only used the first 16 bars.
Topic of Song: diversity is richer;

67. <u>Nonviolence May Take a Long Time</u>:
This Secular Hymn is built on the song "Redeemed", written by William James Kirkpatrick in 1882. The hymn "Redeemed" [#268 in the Christian Life Hymnal] is the source that I used.
Topic of Song: nonviolence;

68. <u>Nonviolence Must Be Taught</u>:
This Secular Hymn is built on the 1911 tune "All in the April Evening" by Scottish composer Hugh S. Roberton. I harmonized the tune and arranged it for SATB to avoid possible copyright infringement. (However I put my arrangement in the public domain so you may copy and perform it without worry.)
Topic of Song: nonviolence, like other important skills, needs to be taught;

69. <u>Nothing's Heavy with Lots of Hands</u>:
This Secular Hymn is built on the 1827 tune "Hendon" by Cesar Malan. Nowadays the tune is better known as the hymn "Take My Life and Let It Be" [#302 in the Christian Life Hymnal], which is the source that I used.
Topic of Song: working together;

70. <u>Oh Child, Do Not Despair</u>:
The original tune (St. Thomas) was written back in the 1760's by Aaron Williams. A number of hymns were written on the St. Thomas tune, including "O Bless the Lord, My Soul" [#35 in the Christian Life Hymnal] and "I Love Thy Kingdom, Lord" [#320 in the Christian Life Hymnal]. However I originally got the melody from the Sacred Harp book - the book of shape-note songs in which the melodies are in the tenor voice instead of the soprano voice. This is why I ended-up writing the arrangement - to get that melody back up into the soprano voice.
Topic of Song: welfare of children;

71. <u>Ojalá</u>:
Pronounced "Oh-ha-LA", this Secular Hymn is based on the traditional hymn "Holy God, We Praise Thy Name" which can be found in a 1686 Catholic songbook and currently as Hymn #39 in the Book of Catholic Worship - 1966 edition (which I used as my source).
Topic of Song: accepting life;

72. <u>Onward, Upward</u>:
This Secular Hymn is built on the song "St. Gertrude", written by Arthur Seymour Sullivan in 1871. It is popularly known today as the hymn "Onward Christian Soldiers" [#438 in the Christian Life Hymnal], which is the source that I used.
Topic of Song: a life of service to others;

73. <u>Open Open Up The Window</u>:
This Secular Hymn is built on the "Austrian Hymn" written by non other than Franz Joseph Hayden in 1797. It is popularly known today by the hymn "Glorious Things of Thee Are Spoken" [#319 in the Christian Life Hymnal] which is the source that I used.
Topic of Song: face the world and learn from it;

74. <u>Our Garden Full of Flowers</u>:
This Secular Hymn is based on the "Passion Chorale" written in 1601 by Leo Hans Hassler. More than a century later, in 1729, it was harmonized by non other than J.S. Bach. Today the tune is sung in the familiar hymn "O Sacred Head, Now Wounded" [#169 in the Christian Life Hymnal], which is the source that I used.
Topic of Song: growing peace;

75. <u>Pain Can Cause</u>:
This Secular Hymn is built on the 1907 song "Adelaide" by George Coles Stebbins. Nowadays the tune is best known as the hymn "Have Thine Own Way, Lord" [#298 in the Christian Life Hymnal], which is the source that I used.
Topic of Song: be slow to judge people;

76. <u>Parents Gone</u>:
This Secular Hymn is built on the old song "Wondrous Love". The haunting melody (in dorian mode) is thought to be hundreds of years old. Our arrangement is from the hymn "What Wondrous Love Is This" [#174 in the Christian Life Hymnal].
Topic of Song: allegiance to parents;

77. <u>Past Performance is No Guarantee</u>:
This Secular Hymn is based on the tune "Mannheim", written by Friedrich Filitz in 1847. It is popularly known today as the Episcopalian hymn "Lead Us Heavenly Father Lead Us" [found at the "hymnary.org" website], which is the source that I used. (I rightly or wrongly repeated the first 4 measures to give the hymn a more user-friendly AABA structure.)
Topic of Song: plan for the future, because that which got us through youth may not work when we are older;

78. <u>Peace Is Not What I Looked For</u>:
This Secular Hymn is based on music written by Charles Crozat Converse in 1868. Today it is popularly known as the hymn "What a Friend We Have in Jesus" [#460 in the Christian Life Hymnal], which is the source that I used.
Topic of Song: peace comes to those who look for it;

NOTES ON THE INDIVIDUAL HYMNS (continued)

79. <u>Peace Like a River</u>:
This hymn was already secular so no changes were made to the words. There are many arrangements of this famous African-American song on the internet. The source I used was Hymn #408 in my Christian Life Hymnal. My only contributions are the chord symbols for the soprano melody and the fun 4th verse (which I had heard before, probably at camp).
Topic of Song: I've got peace, love and joy like a river;

80. <u>People are More</u>:
This secular hymn is built on the hard-to-spell tune "Aberystwyth", written by Joseph Parry in 1879. It is more commonly known today as the hymn "Jesus Lover of My Soul [#395 in the Christian Life Hymnal], which is the source that I used.
Topic of Song: we tend to imprison people with labels;

81. <u>People We Need to Meet</u>:
This Secular Hymn is based on a Silesian folksong. It is popularly known today as the hymn "Fairest Lord Jesus" [#53 in the Christian Life Hymnal], which is the source that I used.
Topic of Song: accepting those we once rejected;

82. <u>People Will Change</u>:
This Secular Hymn is based on the 1685 German chorale "Lobe Den Herren" by Joachim Neander. It is popularly known today as the hymn "Praise to the Lord" [#11 in the Christian Life Hymnal], which is the source that I used.
Topic of Song: people change whether they know it or not; we must hold on to them;

83. <u>Relieving Suffering</u>:
This Secular Hymn is built on the song "Need", written by Robert Lowry in 1872. The tune is commonly known today as "I Need Thee Every Hour" [#459 in the Christian Life Hymnal], which is the source that I used.
Topic of Song: relieving suffering in others;

84. <u>Rise and Shine</u>:
This Secular Hymn comes from an old 1825 pentatonic tune called "Holy Manna". (Pentatonic songs are built on 5-note scales. They can be played using only the black keys of the piano. To my ear these tunes are special and have a Chinese flavor to them.) The hymn "Brethren, We Have Met to Worship" [#581 in the Christian Life Hymnal] is built on this tune and is the source that I used.
Topic of Song: motivational;

85. <u>Seen, Heard and Understood</u>:
This Secular Hymn is based on the tune "Bethany", written by Lowell Mason in 1856. It is known today as the hymn "Nearer, My God, to Thee" [#426 in the Christian Life Hymnal], which is the source that I used.
Topic of Song: needs of others;

86. <u>Skating, Skating</u>:
This Secular Hymn is built on "Westminster Abbey", written by Henry Purcell around 1680. It is more commonly known today as the hymn "Christ is Made the Sure Foundation" [#318 in the Christian Life Hymnal], which is the source that I used.
Topic of Song: making mistakes is healthy;

87. <u>So Many Ways</u>:
This Secular Hymn is built on the 1912 tune "Billing" by Sir Richard Runciman Terry. It is more commonly known today as the hymn "Praise to the Holiest in the Height". The score can be found online at hymnary.org (which is the source that I used).
Topic of Song: choosing to live our lives to reduce suffering;

88. <u>Some Are Young, Some Old</u>:
This Secular Hymn is based on the hymn "Will Your Anchor Hold" or "We Have An Anchor", written by William James Kirkpatrick in 1882 [#423 in the Christian Life Hymnal], which is the source that I used.
Topic of Song: we have to accept that a natural community has a wide assortment of people;

89. <u>Someday When Guns Are Gone</u>:
This Secular Hymn is built on the tune "Dennis" by Johann Georg Nageli. It was arranged by Lowell Mason in 1845. It is popularly known today as the hymn "Blest Be The Tie That Binds" [#334 in the Christian Life Hymnal], which I used as my source. (I added an extra bar at measures 3 and 6 to prolong the held pitches. This regularizes the structure and reflects how the hymn is actually sung in practice.)
Topic of Song: future generations will look back in horror at our use of guns;

90. <u>Someone Should</u>:
This Secular Hymn is built on the strangely spelled Welsh tune "Cwm Rhondda", composed in 1905 by John Hughes. However our source is a later hymn titled "Guide Me, O Thou Great Jehovah" [#413 in the Christian Life Hymnal].
Topic of Song: supporting community;

91. <u>Spent Our Treasure</u>:
This secular hymn is based on the traditional African-American spiritual "Were You There". It can be found as Hymn #161 in the Christian Life Hymnal and can also be found online at hymnary.org (which is the source that I used).
Topic of Song: the money we spend on weapons could allow our schools and health care services to flourish;

92. <u>Standing At Bat</u>:
This Secular Hymn is built on the 1824 song "Hamburg" by Lowell Mason. This is a very simple tune, using only 5 pitches. It is popularly known today as the hymn "When I Survey the Wondrous Cross" [#171 in the Christian Life Hymnal] which is the source that I used.
Topic of Song: stepping out of your group;

93. <u>Step by Step</u>:
This Secular Hymn is built on the tune "China", written by William Batchelder Bradbury in 1862. It is quite popularly known today as the hymn "Jesus Loves Me, This I Know" [#274 in the Christian Life Hymnal], which is the source that I used.
Topic of Song: unrelenting pursuit of goals should be balanced with other things;

94. <u>Storms Will Come</u>:
This Secular Hymn is based on the hymn tune "St. Helen", written by Sir George C Martin in 1889. It is more commonly known today as the hymn "Lord Enthroned in Heavenly Splendor". The hymn score can be found online at musescore.com and at other sites.
Topic of Song: storms are sure to come - but storms are also sure to go;

95. <u>Striving To Be</u>:
This Secular Hymn is based on the tune "Pentecost", written by William Boyd in 1868. It is popularly known today as the hymn "Fight the Good Fight" (which was used in the film "Chariots of Fire"). The source I used was found online at cyberhymnal.org.
Topic of Song: striving to be poor instead of wealthy;

96. <u>Swapping Shoes</u>:
This Secular Hymn is built on the curiously-named tune "Dix" written by Conrad Kocher in 1838 (and arranged by William Henry Monk in 1865). It is more commonly known today as the hymns "Praise to God, Immortal Praise" [#595 in the Christian Life Hymnal] and "For the Beauty of the Earth" [#171 in the Christian Life Hymnal] which is the source I used.
Topic of Song: by putting ourselves into someone else's predicament, we learn that we would act the same;

97. <u>Tall Oaks From Little Acorns Grow</u>:
This Secular Hymn is built on the traditional Irish melody "St. Columba". It was harmonized by Charles Villiers Stanford in 1906. It is popularly known today as the hymn "The King of Love My Shepherd Is" [#370 in the Christian Life Hymnal] which is the source that I used.
Topic of Song: friendships often begin with the word "Hello";

98. <u>The Greatest Walk</u>:
This Secular Hymn is based on the tune "Jerusalem", a 1916 anthem written by Sir Hubert Parry. It was written to a poem by William Blake which began: "And did those feet in ancient time walk upon England's mountains green?" That subject matter is undoubtedly why it was sung by a choir at the end of "Chariots of Fire" (a 1981 movie about runners in the 1924 Olympics). It's also why our Secular Hymn is about "walking". Parry wrote it as a unison song, not as an SATB arrangement. It is a favorite song in England and is sung in Anglican and some Episcopalian churches. However I was unable to find any SATB arrangement that was not under copyright protection, so I created my own arrangement (and put it in the public domain).
Topic of Song: accepting others;

99. <u>The Many Truths</u>:
This Secular Hymn is built on a tune used in "Finlandia" by Sibelius. It was subsequently used in the hymn "Be Still My Soul" [#364 in the Christian Life Hymnal]. However that arrangement is still under copyright protection, so I created my own arrangement (and put it in the public domain).
Topic of Song: accepting others;

100. <u>The Only Path to Peace is Peace</u>:
This Secular Hymn is based on the tune "St. Anne", written by William Croft in 1708. It is more commonly known today as the hymn "Our God Our Help in Ages Past" [which can be found at the online site "openhymnal.org"], which is the source that I used.
Topic of Song: "fighting" for peace has a history of failure; "peace-ing" for peace must be our strategy;

101. <u>Them Over There</u>:
The source of this Secular Hymn is "Lasst Uns Erfreuen" (pre-1623). It was harmonized by Ralph Vaughan Williams in 1906. It is most popular today as the hymn "All Creatures Of Our God and King". However the hymn "From All That Dwell Below the Skies" [#19 in the Christian Life Hymnal] is the source that I used.
Topic of Song: seeing others as ourselves;

102. There Are Times:
This Secular Hymn is built on the 1868 song "All to Christ" by John Thomas Grape. It is known today as the hymn "Jesus Paid It All" [#265 in the Christian Life Hymnal] which is the source that I used.
Topic of Song: loss of identity through medication, drugs etc.

103. There is a Game:
This Secular Hymn is built on a hymn written by William Augustine Ogden in 1885, titled "Bring Them In", [#361 in the Christian Life Hymnal], which is the source that I used.
Topic of Song: behavior beyond control;

104. There is a Rule of Thumb:
This Secular Hymn is built on the song "Diademata" written by George Elvey back in the 1860's. The name "Diademata" comes from the Greek word for "crown". So it's not surprising that the most popular hymn written on this tune is titled: "Crown Him With Many Crowns" [#46 in the Christian Life Hymnal], which is the source that I used.
Topic of Song: acceptance of life;

105. There is an Empty Box:
This Secular Hymn is built on the tune "Aurelia", written by Samuel Sebastian Wesley is 1864. It is more commonly known today as the hymn "The Church's One Foundation" [#316 in the Christian Life Hymnal], which is the source that I used.
Topic of Song: we must preserve that which others consider meaningful and beautiful;

106. There is Something Wrong:
This Secular Hymn is built from the hymn "The Old Rugged Cross" written by George Bennard in 1913. The source I used was the Christian Life Hymnal (Hymn #167).
Topic of Song: "Killing the Bad Guy" is an ugly game;

107. There's a Better Way:
This Secular Hymn is built on the tune "Blessed Name", a 19th century American camp meeting melody. It was arranged by Ralph Erskine Hudson in 1887. The source I used is the hymn "Blessed Be The Name" [#37 in the Christian Life Hymnal].
Topic of Song: peace, anti-gun;

108. There's a Road Between Our Lands:
This Secular Hymn is built on a 17th century English melody titled "Royal Oak", which is recognized today as the popular hymn "All Things Bright and Beautiful" [#243 in the Christian Life Hymnal], which is the source that I used. It was arranged for choir in 1915 by Martin Shaw.
Topic of Song: even very different people have common interests that they can share;

109. There's Claim Number One:
This Secular Hymn is based on the hymn "Revive Us Again", written by John Jenkins Husband around 1815. I found it as Hymn #338 in my Christian Life Hymnal, which is the source that I used.
Topic of Song: sometimes we have to decide between two claims that are both true;

110. There's More Than One Way:
This Secular Hymn is built on the tune "Hanover", written by William Croft in 1708. Today it is more commonly known as the hymn "Ye Servants of God" [#209 in the Christian Life Hymnal] which is the source that I used.
Topic of Song: since there are many ways to live our lives, we should give the deviants some room;

111. <u>Things Are The Way They Are</u>:
This Secular Hymn is based on the tune "Nun Danket", written by Johann Crueger in 1647. It is popularly known today as the hymn "Now Thank We All Our God". The available E-flat arrangement (by Felix Mendelssohn, I believe) had a rather high tessitura for the sopranos and some really low bass notes (E-flat). I try to avoid such low notes because few can sing them with any power. So I lowered the key to "D" and made a simpler, more user-friendly arrangement and put it in the public domain.
Topic of Song: things will remain as they are unless we make changes;

112. <u>This Day, This Day</u>:
This Secular Hymn is built on the music "Sine Nomine", composed by Ralph Vaughan Williams in 1906. It is popularly known today as the hymn "For All The Saints" [#547 in the Christian Life Hymnal], which is the source that I used.
Topic of Song: living one day at a time;

113. <u>Tick-Tock</u>:
This Secular Hymn is built on the tune "Regent Square", written by Henry Thomas Smart in 1867. The tune is more commonly known today by several hymns: "Angels From the Realms of Glory" [#98 in the Christian Life Hymnal], "Christ is Made the Sure Foundation" [#317 in the Christian Life Hymnal], and finally the source that I used: "Lo He Comes With Clouds Descending" [#210 in the Christian Life Hymnal].
Topic of Song: accepting "time";

114. <u>'Tis a Gift</u>:
This Secular Hymn is built on the very familiar Shaker song "Simple Gifts", written by Joseph Bracket in 1848. The melody was popularized even more when Aaron Copland used it in his 1944 ballet "Appalachian Spring". I created the SATB arrangement and put it in the public domain.
Topic of Song: 'tis a gift to be simple;

115. <u>To Find a Place</u>:
This Secular Hymn is built on the tune "Crucifer" written by Sydney Hugo Nicholson in 1916. Today it is more commonly known by the hymn "Lift High the Cross" [#203 in the Christian Life Hymnal], which is the source that I used.
Topic of Song: the importance of having a home and community;

116. <u>To Live Our Lives Addiction-Free</u>:
This Secular Hymn is based on the 1753 tune "Deus Tuorum Militum" (the God of your soldiers). The tune is better known today by hymns such as: "O Love How Deep", "The Lord is King, Lift Up Thy Voice", "Ring Out the Old, Ring In the New", "What Thanks and Praise to Thee We Owe", and the source that I used from the website hymnary.org: "Bless Thou the Gifts".
Topic of Song: protecting ourselves from addictive substances will give us a kind of freedom;

117. <u>To Make the World a Better Place</u>:
This Secular Hymn is built on a tune by William Horsley in 1830. Today it is popularly known by the hymns "Majestic Sweetness Sits Enthroned" [#200 in the Christian Life Hymnal] and "There is a Green Hill Far Away" [#160 in the Christian Life Hymnal] which is the source I used.
Topic of Song: hiring someone different than you is very important;

118. <u>To Soldiers Lost</u>:
This Secular Hymn is based on the traditional Irish melody "St. Patrick's Breastplate". The melody is more commonly known today as the hymn "I Bind Unto Myself Today" [#6 in the Christian Life Hymnal], which is the source that I used. The source is a unison work, so I made the SATB arrangement myself and put it in the public domain.
Topic of Song: any social problems that veterans have is of our own making and is therefore our responsibility to solve;

119. <u>To Those Who Came Before</u>:
This Secular Hymn is based on the 1906 tune "Down Ampney" by Ralph Vaughan Williams. "Down Ampney" is the town in which Ralph Vaughan Williams was born (on October 12, 1872). It is more commonly known today as the hymn "Come Down O Love Divine" [#216 in the Christian Life Hymnal], which is the source that I used.
Topic of Song: we stand on foundations built by others;

120. <u>Today Is My Day</u>:
This Secular Hymn is based on the 1887 hymn "Trust and Obey" by Daniel Brink Towner [#504 in the Christian Life Hymnal] which is the source that I used. I added an extra bar after measures 7 and 15 to extend the held pitch. This regularizes the structure and notates the hymn the way it is actually sung in practice.
Topic of Song: working towards goals can help stave-off despair ;

121. <u>Today's the Day</u>:
This Secular Hymn is built on the tune "Darwall's 148th" written by John Darwall in 1770. It is more popularly known today as the hymns: "Rejoice, The Lord Is King" [#206 in the Christian Life Hymnal] and "Join All The Glorious Names" [#43 in the Christian Life Hymnal], both of which I used as sources.
Topic of Song: making a resolution to change;

122. <u>Together For So Long</u>:
This Secular Hymn is built on the old tune "Lenox" written by Lewis Edson in 1748. The familiar hymn "Arise, My Soul, Arise!" is also built on the "Lenox" tune and is the source that I used.
Topic of Song: communication;

123. <u>T'wards a World That Has No Guns</u>:
This Secular Hymn is built on Beethoven's 1824 song "Hymn to Joy" from his Ninth Symphony. It was adapted in 1864 by Edward Hodges. Today it appears in hymns such as "Joyful, Joyful, We Adore Thee" [#235 in the Christian Life Hymnal] or "Alleluia, Alleluia! Hearts to Heaven [#190 in the Christian Life Hymnal], which is the source that I used.
Topic of Song: peace, anti-gun;

124. <u>Trusting You, Trusting Me</u>:
This Secular Hymn is built on the famous "Largo" theme from Antonin Dvorak's 1893 "New World" symphony. It is popularly known today as the song "Going Home". I could find no copyright-free SATB arrangements of this song so I arranged it myself and put it into the public domain.
Topic of Song: so much of life depends on "trust";

125. <u>Ultimately We May Not Have Free Will</u>:
This Secular Hymn is based on the old French melody "Noël Nouvelet", which can be found online at the website "chanted.com". It is only found as a unison song, so I harmonized it and arranged it for SATB choir.
Topic of Song: many of us understand that we don't have a "free will" and feel that our punitive prisons and our hero-worship is unfair. (Sales Pitch: I wrote a fictional book about a community of determinists with the title "Aren't We The Lucky Ones" which is still available);

126. <u>Unconscious Bias</u>:
This Secular Hymn is based on the tune "Ebenezer", written by Thomas John Williams in 1890. The tune is better known today by many hymns, including "Come O Spirit, Dwell Among Us", Thy Strong Word Did Cleave the Darkness", "Ton-y-Botel", "O the Deep, Deep Love of Jesus", "Once to Every Man and Nation", and "Singing Songs of Expectation" [#321 in the Christian Life Hymnal], which is the source that I used.
Topic of Song: we should be mindful of our unconscious biases;

127. <u>Unless There's No-One Watching</u>:
This Secular Hymn is built on the song "Endless Song" by Robert Lowry in 1860. It is popularly known today as "How Can I Keep From Singing" [#509 in the Christian Life Hymnal], which is the source that I used.
Topic of Song: relieving suffering in others;

128. <u>Wake, Awake</u>:
This Secular Hymn is built on the 1599 German tune "Wachet Auf" by Philipp Nicolai. J. S. Bach subsequently harmonized it and used it in a cantata, which is the source that I used.
Topic of Song: motivational;

129. <u>Walking in Someone's Shoes</u>:
This Secular Hymn is built on a Silesian melody and was arranged by Joseph Roff in 1842. Today the tune is best known by the hymn "O God of Loveliness" [#59 in the Book of Catholic Worship - 1966 Edition], which is the source that I used.
Topic of Song: understanding and accepting others;

130. <u>We Are People, Plastic People</u>:
This Secular Hymn is built on the hymn "Angel Voices Ever Singing", written by Edwin G. Monk in 1861. It can be found online at the website "openhymnal.org", which is the source that I used.
Topic of Song: it's not the people, it's the *situations* that they are put into that shape them into the characters that they are;

131. <u>We Are Searching</u>:
This Secular Hymn is based on the 1886 hymn written by Peter Philip Bilhorn titled "I Will Sing the Wondrous Story" [#507 in the Christian Life Hymnal], which is the source that I used.
Topic of Song: "searching" for answers is often more rewarding than "finding" the answers;

132. <u>We Can Be Tolerant</u>:
This Secular Hymn is built on a traditional Irish melody titled "Slane". It is popularly known today as the hymn "Be Thou My Vision" [#386 in the Christian Life Hymnal]. However that arrangement is still under copyright protection, so I reharmonized the melody, created a new arrangement, and put it in the public domain.
Topic of Song: a test of true tolerance;

133. <u>We Can Get Things To Happen</u>:
This Secular Hymn is built on the popular African-American spiritual "Let Us Break Bread Together". Since I could find no arrangements of this song that were copyright-free, I made the SATB arrangement myself and put it in the public domain.
Topic of Song: people working together can get things done;

134. <u>We Mean "Will You Love Me?"</u>:
This Secular Hymn is built on the hymn "My Jesus I Love Thee I Know Thou Art Mine", written by Adoniram Judson Gordon in 1876. It is Hymn #61 in the Christian Life Hymnal, which is the source that I used.
Topic of Song: everything we say can be translated into "Will You Love Me?"

135. <u>We're Not Alone</u>:
This Secular Hymn is based on a very famous Irish melody. Although it may be familiar to some as the hymn "I Cannot Tell", it is known throughout the world as the folksong "Londonderry Air" or "Danny Boy". The tune can be found online at the "cyberhymnal" website (which is the source that I used). Since an SATB arrangement was not available, I arranged it myself and put it into the public domain.
Topic of Song: we're not alone as long as our nonhuman companions are alive and well;

136. <u>We're Not At Our Best</u>:
This Secular Hymn is built on the Welsh melody "St. Denio" which was adapted and harmonized by John Roberts in 1839. It is more commonly known today as the hymn "Immortal, Invisible, God Only Wise" [#18 in the Christian Life Hymnal], which is the source that I used;
Topic of Song: "fear" is a crippling emotion from which we must escape;

137. <u>We're Parents of a Soldier</u>:
This Secular Hymn is built on an old American camp-meeting tune, but it is very popularly known today as the "Battle Hymn of the Republic" [#603 in the Christian Life Hymnal], which is the source that I used.
Topic of Song: we are all parents of soldiers - but probably not good parents;

138. <u>What Are We Doing?</u>
This Secular Hymn is based on a melody from George Frederick Handel's 1747 oratorio "Macchabaeus". Among the hymns based on this tune is "Thine Be the Glory" [#188 in the Christian Life Hymnal], which was the source I used.
Topic of Song: acceptance of life / human condition;

139. <u>When Feeling Lost</u>:
This Secular Hymn is built on the traditional English melody "Kingsfold". It was arranged and harmonized by Ralph Vaughan Williams in 1906. It is more commonly heard today in the hymns "I Heard the Voice of Jesus Say" [#530 in the Christian Life Hymnal] and "O Sing a Song of Bethlehem" [#146 in the Christian Life Hymnal].
Topic of Song: it is healthful to learn new things and meet new people;

140. <u>When I Am Down</u>:
This Secular Hymn is built on the traditional African-American spiritual "Down To The River To Pray". Even though it has the conventional number of measures (16, or in this case 32) it feels to me curiously off-balance - enticingly off-balance - as if there are the right number of boxes but they are filled unevenly. I could find no SATB arrangements and so arranged it myself. This tune was used in the film "O Brother, Where Art Thou?"
Topic of Song: walking and talking can be a healing combination;

141. <u>When Playing Cards</u>:
This Secular Hymn is built on the old song *O Store Gud* which I obtained from a 1903 Swedish songbook. The tune is popularly known today as "How Great Thou Art". The 1903 arrangement was not pleasing to me and the newer "How Great Thou Art" arrangement was still under copyright protection, so I wrote a new SATB arrangement and put it into the public domain.
Topic of Song: tolerance, accepting others;

142. <u>Who's My Neighbor?</u>
This Secular Hymn is built on the tune "Victory" by none other than Palestrina in 1588. It was arranged in 1861 by William Henry Monk. It is popularly known today as the hymn "The Strife is O'er" [#191 in the Christian Life Hymnal] which is the source that I used.
Topic of Song: our neighbors are those in need, whether near or far;

143. <u>Why Does This Phrase Have Five Measures?</u>
This Secular Hymn is built on the tune "Lauda Anima", written by John Goss in 1869. It is popularly known today as the hymn "Praise My Soul the King of Heaven" [#12 in the Christian Life Hymnal], which is the source that I used.
Topic of Song: all music has unexplored depths;

144. <u>You Took the One Road</u>:
This Secular Hymn is built on the traditional Scottish folk song "Loch Lomand", which the world knows by lyrics that go something like: "Oh, you take the high road and I'll take the low road and I'll be in Scotland before you". I arranged it for SATB choir and put it into the public domain.
Topic of Song: different people taking very different roads just might turn out the same at the end;

Recent Works by Secretary Michael

Jo Puma - Wild Choir Music
Collection of 36 traditional "Sacred Harp" arrangements with new secular lyrics for our diverse society. This collection has removed the 3 barriers that have kept this music out of our schools: inappropriate lyrics, poor shape-note legibility, and nonstandard use of standard solfege names. Now we all have a chance to experience this exciting early American music. (Book available; free download not yet available)

Secular Hymnal
Collection of 144 favorite hymn tunes from around the world. The hymn tunes have been re-notated and given thoughtful egalitarian lyrics that promote peace. Many public schools use them for choral sight-reading practice. Available in both unison/guitar and SATB choir editions. Now we all have a chance to share in these musical treasures. (Books available; free downloads available;)

Twimfina
A peace-themed musical play for singing groups of all ages. The story is about a young woman named "Twimfina" (an acronym for "The World Is My Family, I'm Not Afraid") who runs off to a hostile country. It is scored for voice and piano. The play is divided into 21 segments, many of which can stand alone. This allows an acting group to perform individual segments instead of the entire 2.5 hour play. (Book available; free download available;)

Lifesongs
A "lifesong" is a 4-movement choral work (with or without instruments) in which a rational argument is battled-out musically. There's only one rule: every lifesong must use the following four titles for its four movements: "Credo" - "One Hand" - "Other Hand" - "Go and Do"
Secretary Michael has begun working on a series of 6 lifesongs, some of which are available now; the rest will become available as they are completed in future years.

Aren't We the Lucky Ones
A book-length story about a group of college science students who share an understanding that people don't truly have a free will. There are no "good people" or "bad people", just lucky and unlucky ones. This insight carries with it the responsibility to protect the "unlucky" from the wrath of the "lucky". The students form a community in order to live out their ideals. (Book available - both paperback and digital).

Joy of Piggyback Songs
Dozens of fun, short choral works in which more than one melody is sung at the same time. Book (and free internet download) will become available after it is completed.

"Artists can change the world by correcting
the misconceptions that divide people.
Artists can also cause the misconceptions.
We're all artists. We all must choose."
-Secretary Michael

www.ingramcontent.com/pod-product-compliance
Lightning Source LLC
Chambersburg PA
CBHW081641040426
42449CB00015B/3408